THE ENGLISH RENAISSANCE

FACT OR FICTION?

THE ENGLISH

RENAISSANCE

FACT OR FICTION?

E. M. W. Tillyard

GREENWOOD PRESS, PUBLISHERS
NEW YORK   **1968**

First Greenwood reprinting, 1968

LIBRARY OF CONGRESS catalogue card number: 68-54441

To Bayard and Margaret Turnbull

Preface

THIS book reproduces with very few changes the Turnbull Memorial Lectures which I had the honor to give at the Johns Hopkins University in the academic year 1950-51. A faithful and appreciative audience was one of the factors that made the giving of them a pleasure. Another was the kindness of the University staff in making me feel at home. These are things one might be lucky enough to encounter elsewhere, but to enjoy the hospitality of the family concerned with founding a lectureship now of over sixty years standing must be an experience one will surely not find readily, if at all, outside Baltimore. And it is an experience I count myself lucky to have had, and for which I am very grateful.

In my section on the lyric I wish to record my debt to Sir Edmund Chambers's essay, *Some Aspects of the Mediaeval Lyric*. This appeared first as an appendix to Chambers and Sidgwick, *Early English Lyrics* and was reprinted in Chambers, *Sir*

Thomas Wyatt and some Collected Studies. Since commenting, in the same section, on the anonymous poem about the maiden on the moor, I wrote a letter to the *Times Literary Supplement* (published May 11, 1951) making a further suggestion about it and appealing for further help in elucidation. The appeal was answered in an interesting letter from R. J. Schoeck of Cornell University.

E. M. W. TILLYARD

Jesus College, Cambridge
November 31, 1951

Contents

Introduction

IN THESE essays Professor Tillyard looks once more at the complex nature of the English Renaissance and considers again the problem of its actuality. His answer is judicious as all answers should be: there are similarities between the artistic characteristics of the English Middle Ages and the times of the Tudors and there are clear differences. Literature is not architecture where the distinctions are sudden and visible to all. It is not sculpture which dates itself immediately. As a child of memory, literature is fabricated of many recollections which are interwoven with shining areas of man's half-forgotten years. It cannot deny time. Hence the English Renaissance looks backward through the annals of British culture just as it throws sideward glances at that of the Continent. In a sense, what is called the English Renaissance may have only been half-born or, perhaps, it was only half-resurrected.

The answer to the question depends on how one reads, and the process of reading depends on much that is intangible. A sure perception of tone—and *tone* is a word that Tillyard uses with justice—is the best instrument of decision, for the alterations between the two periods cannot be explained so well by intellectual coloration as by emotional emphases. Ideas and myths, the clothing of ideas, have a tendency to remain static; it is the fervor with which they are embraced or rejected, modified or perverted, that makes the pattern. In the case of the Renaissance, fervor is a synonym for art. Tillyard, it seems to me, has employed this method with the utmost skill and fairness. Yet his task was no easy one. A century of scholarship lies behind the problems of his book and he was forced to consider it and place his case beside it. I can, therefore, think of no better way to introduce these essays than to describe the wealth of discussion that preceded them in order to suggest how modestly and adroitly the Master of Jesus College has taken up the threads of the debate.

Though the men of the Renaissance were not unconscious of what they were doing and though they were quite able to use expressions like " renatae literae " or " rinascita di queste arti sino al secolo che noi viviamo," it was not until the latter part of the eighteenth century that the concept of a distinct movement became fixed. At that time the Renaissance was thought of as a reaction against barbarism, but a reaction that was not entirely successful. Warton, for instance, defends Milton's " Lycidas " against the strictures of Johnson by apologizing for the milieu in which it was written. " Our poetry was not yet purged of its Gothic combinations." With the publication in 1855 of the first volume of Jules Michelet's *Renaissance et Temps Modernes,* the serious consideration of the nature of this new and exciting movement in human culture begins.

Michelet's thesis was expanded in Jacob Burckhardt's *Die Kultur der Renaissance in Italien,* a book in which culture in terms of art and literature almost goes without mention. Burckhardt thought of the Renaissance as different from the Middle Ages in its social and political organizations, in its emphasis on the individual and the broad world—broad in both space and time—that lay before the new egocentric, and in its a-religiosity. Like his predecessor Voigt, Burckhardt held that the Renaissance began in Italy and that it owed its necessary impetus to the rediscovery of classical antiquity. Burckhardt had many disciples. One of them was J. A. Symonds, whose series of informative essays between 1875 and 1886 fail to give us a unified portrait but, nevertheless, provide us with impressive glimpses not only of the Renaissance but of the author's own peculiar prejudices. Another disciple was Gebhart, whose *Les Origines de la Renaissance en Italie,* 1879, stresses the theory that in Italian ground and in Italian ground alone was the soil rich enough—and with moisture of the right quantity—for the full blooming of this modern flower.

All of these scholars were convinced that the Renaissance was quite different and quite separate from the Middle Ages and that it could have had its inception only in Italy. As commentaries on this dogma, other studies were written explaining how this new cultural movement wandered to other lands. The best of these are Geiger's *Humanismus und Renaissance in Italien und Deutschland* and Müntz's *La Renaissance en Italie et en France*. The nineteenth century was mainly engaged in elaborating the theses of Burckhardt, but his conclusions were not to remain unquestioned for long.

The attack on these nineteenth-century contentions was of a triple nature. There were those who held that the Renaissance was simply a continuation and enlargement of certain aspects of the Middle Ages. To the proof of this theory, certain men of the Middle Ages were pushed forward as having all the characteristics of men of the Renaissance. Walter Pater with his championing of Abelard may be regarded as the patron of this new point of view, though Pater in no way confused the Renaissance and the Middle Ages. A contemporary of Pater, Henry Thode, went much further in this direction when he revealed St. Francis as a typical example of the Renaissance Christian humanist. His theory, in this respect, was endorsed in 1939 by Douglas Bush in *The Renaissance and English Humanism*. Karl Burdach proposed a less saintly figure. In his *Reformation, Renaissance, Humanismus*, 1918, he described Petrarch's friend Rienzo as one of the earliest protagonists of the new ideals. Other scholars offered other candidates. The search for proto-Renaissance men has now become such a scholar's pastime and so many obscure humanists, Latin poets, and amateurs of antiquities have been exhumed from the depths of the so-called Middle Ages that the calendar begins to be crowded.

A second theory of Burckhardt's that has come under attack and one that Symonds elaborated with protestant vigor is the paganism of that culture. Browning's Bishop of St. Praxed's is the poetical product of this theory. The non-Christian nature of the Renaissance was explored to some degree by Neumann in his *Byzantinische Kultur und Renaissance Kultur* and stressed by Müntz in *Precursori e Propugnatori del Rinascimento*, a book that tells us much about the pagan inspiration of Renaissance art. Both Thode and Burdach as well as Bush and Toffanin disagree with this position and it has been vigorously assailed by Zabughin in his *Storia del Rinascimento Cristiano in Italia*. The Renaissance is now definitely established as Christian in its inception and this is likely to be the continued attitude.

The third objection to the theories of Burckhardt was the most violent because it appealed to the fetish of national pride. Neumann had attempted to argue as early as 1903 that the origins of the Renaissance were Gothic, but at that time his remarks made little or no impression. Then, in 1929, Nordstrom, who had no deep affection for the Italians, published a book in which he asserted that the notion that the Renaissance began in Italy rested more on Burckhardt than on facts. For him the Renaissance began in France in the twelfth century and to French culture is owed all that subsequently became visible in Petrarch, Boccaccio, and Ariosto. To the French this was a most welcome suggestion. Chamard, the author of *Les Origines de la Poésie Française de la Renaissance*, 1932, thought that the literature of the French Middle Ages produced that of the French Renaissance. Funck-Brentano went somewhat beyond this when he suggested that the Renaissance might have had a richer culture if the Italian movement described by Burckhardt had not interfered with the exfoliation of French mediaeval culture.

There is something to be said for these opinions if one limits one's theories to historical first impressions. The cultural center of Europe in the Middle Ages was certainly France. Dante has almost no Italian predecessors, and talk as we will about the poetical schools of Umbria, Bologna, and Tuscany, we are always forced to admit that Petrarch looks towards Provence. In almost all the arts Italy was second to France. The historian of philosophy will point to Lanfranc, Anselm, Peter Lombard, Aquinas, and Bonaventura, but he must likewise admit that it was in France that they studied and taught. We must also grant that there is a tonal difference between the twelfth century in France and the Quattrocento.

The theories of Nordstrom, Chamard, and Funck-Brentano were attacked by Italo Siciliano, who wisely pointed out in his *Medio Evo e Rinascimento*, 1936, that there now seemed to be a whole procession of Renaissances—a Byzantine Renaissance, an Irish Renaissance, an Old English Renaissance, a Carolingian Renaissance, an Ottonian Renaissance, a Suabian Renaissance, a French Renaissance, and a Norman Renaissance. It is as Neri stated in *La Rinascita Medievale*: " The Renaissances shine like fools' fires from the distant regions of the past." Siciliano argues most cogently that Rome, after all, so dominated the Middle Ages that Italy really never left the stage. There was, he thinks, a " Romance Middle Age " between the Middle Ages and the Renaissance which was both French and Italian. Its manifestations in the two countries differed in tempo and duration, but it reached its peak in Italy in the fifteenth and sixteenth centuries.

The last important essay is by Bush and it prepares the way for these lectures. The terms " mediaeval " and " Renaissance " are for Bush unhistoric and he sees the two periods as parts of a cultural parade and not as totally separate movements. The whole pressure of culture can best be described in terms of Christian Humanism which is a fairly continuous thing. Bush finds that this aspect of the Renaissance had its counterpart in England and that the literature of the Tudor and Stuart periods owed much to the ethical and metaphysical thought of the English humanists. The apex of the movement for Bush comes in the poetry of Milton, whom he considers to be the last true exponent of Christian humanism in England. It is at this point in the discussion that Tillyard begins.

DON CAMERON ALLEN

THE ENGLISH RENAISSANCE

FACT OR FICTION?

I

The Renaissance

"THE English Renaissance: Fact or Fiction?"— that is the emphatic and apparently ambitious title I have chosen for this series of essays. But titles should be emphatic, and as a title the one I have chosen is better than, for instance, "Some Notes on the Transition from Medieval to Renaissance Ways of Thought as Exemplified in Certain Classes of English Literature." But though rightly emphatic my title may well arouse expectations which these essays will not in fact fulfill; and before I enter my theme I had better warn the reader of one thing he is not to expect. My subject has little to do with the history of ideas. Any ideas I discuss are simple and generally allowed to have existed in the period of time under review; anything new I have to say will belong to the region of literary criticism, not to that of the history of ideas.

Nevertheless, though I am little concerned with the detailed evolution of man's ideas in past epochs, what I have to say concerning certain pieces of literature in the Middle Ages and the Renaissance in England is colored and perhaps held together by a distinct notion. In my earlier writing, though trying to be fair, I have had foremost in my mind the possible continuity between the two epochs: now, to adjust the balance, I have foremost in my mind, though still trying to be fair, the differences between them.

My scheme is to begin by setting forth in a very general way certain large differences between medieval and Renaissance habits of thought in England; and to go on thence to test and illustrate these differences in three widely separated areas of literature: the lyric, the epic, and literary criticism. I have aimed at a rather difficult target, a mean between the popular and the academic; and perhaps I have not achieved perfect consistency. My sections on the epic and literary criticism are probably a little more on the academic side than the rest.

If one could have questioned a typical Victorian of the later nineteenth century on the Renaissance, the result would have been somewhat as follows. The Renaissance was a manifestation of new life, an outburst of virtuous floridity after the cramping restraints and withering asceticisms of the Middle Ages. In this Victorian's mind the movement would be connected generally and principally with Italy and would carry with it specific, if little formulated, associations with Florence and Amalfi, carnivals and poisonings, orange trees and red wines, the Brownings, honeymoons by Lake Como, and churches and galleries full of highly colored paintings. Yes, pictures above everything. To a Victorian the word Renaissance itself was intoxicating; but when, to vary the metaphor, the mud it had stirred up in the mind had begun to settle, what grew clear was that the Renaissance was a great effusion of art. From its faint and primitive beginnings in Cimabue and Giotto painting progressed through Fra Angelico, Botticelli, and Perugino to its unquestioned climax in Leonardo da Vinci, Michelangelo, and Raphael, with Titian and the other Venetians as a magnificent and only slightly inferior sideshow. Of the three, Raphael was the age's darling; and the Dresden Madonna was the greatest picture in the world.

Then, of course, there were the classics. The Middle Ages had been barbarous enough to forget Greek; and when it was recovered, people grew very excited; and of course quite rightly. Our Victorian might be vague on what precise form the excitement took; only he believed it arose very quickly and he was certain that it was a very good thing.

Alongside this orthodoxy there were the advanced ideas connected with Rossetti and his circle. Some more daring folk put the climax a little earlier. Great as Leonardo and Raphael and Michelangelo were, there was something more "too too" about

5

Botticelli. One of such folk was Gilbert's young man in Bunthorne's song in *Patience*:

> *A Japanese young man,*
> *A blue and white young man,*
> *A Francesca da Rimini*
> *Niminy Piminy*
> Je ne sais quoi *young man.*

But these amateurs of the slightly archaic never questioned the virtue of the Renaissance; they merely shifted the flowering a little farther back. Or rather they had a different taste in stages of flowering. The rose was all right in itself; only some people (the more refined and sensitive) preferred the still-opening bud to the full-flaunting flower.

Such, crudely indicated, was the popular opinion in the later nineteenth century and it was continued well into the twentieth. Take, for instance, the sentences which begin Miss Sichel's book on the Renaissance in the Home University Library:

Michael Angelo's great painting of the newly created Adam on the ceiling of the Sistine Chapel might be taken as a symbol of the Renaissance, of the time when man was, as it were, re-created more glorious than before, with a body naked and unashamed, and a strong arm, unimpaired by fasting, outstretched towards life and light. Definitions are generally misleading, and it is easier to represent the Renaissance by a symbol than to define it. It was a movement, a revival of man's powers, a reawakening of the consciousness of himself and of the universe.

There is no mistaking the tone of this passage. The authoress is comfortably assured of an audience prejudiced in favor of this "revival of man's powers" and against that suppression of them it assumed to have been the rule in the Middle Ages.

Please remember that I have been speaking of popular not of academic or specialist opinion about the Middle Ages and Renaissance, and about English not American opinion. It may be that Henry Adams's *Mont-Saint-Michel and Chartres*, so little known in England compared with his *Education of Henry Adams*, with its wonderful sense of flowering life in the thirteenth century, had its counterpart in American popular opinion. But this book was not printed (and then only privately) till 1904; and I expect that, in the nineteenth century at least, popular opinion in America was similar to the English.

Now when a gross popular error exists, it is bound to be corrected with a violence which in revulsion breaks through the central core of truth and ends nearly as far from it as before, only on the other side. In the last thirty years people have grown far more interested in the Middle Ages; and some of them have been unable to dissociate that interest from a hostility to the age that followed. The interest has been artistic, philosophical, economic; and I will give two instances of the engendered hostility.

In 1914 Clive Bell published a book called *Art*,

a slick and confident piece of iconoclasm attacking the whole validity of Renaissance art. With a number of others Bell had come to admire the rigors and abstractions of Byzantine art, of such great works as the later mosaics at Ravenna and at Daphni near Athens, and, taking as a norm something little realistic and representational, proceeded to destroy the old hierarchies and to erect a new set, in what for some people was a spirit quite intoxicatingly daring. On the old scheme there had been two supreme ages: that of Phidias and the Parthenon and that of the already mentioned Big Three of the early sixteenth century in Italy. According to Clive Bell there was an apex in the eighth century B.C. and an even greater one in the sixth century A.D. lasting for six centuries and spanning the so-called Dark Ages. Giotto was the last (and by no means the highest) peak in this ridge, and after him an awful decadence set in till the sudden surge-up of the French Impressionists in the second half of the nineteenth century.

More serious were the attacks on the Renaissance as lacking spirituality, as being grossly sensual and human. As a man once influential in my own university of Cambridge I choose for example T. E. Hulme, translator of Sorel and powerful critical force in the group of Imagist poets. Hulme included the Renaissance and the Romantic Revival in one great and vicious mental trend: the trend of ignoring original sin and arrogating to the human spirit more than its due, of grabbing impiously for man those things that essentially belong to God. Hulme sees in an earlier age an opinion of man quite hostile to this one; and of the two opinions he wrote as follows, as recorded in his collected notes published posthumously by Herbert Read under the title of *Speculations*:

The thoroughness with which these two conceptions of man penetrate the life of their respective periods can be illustrated by the difference between their arts. . . . Renaissance art we may call a " vital " art in that it depends on pleasure in the reproduction of human and natural forms. Byzantine art is the exact contrary of this. There is nothing vital in it; the emotion you get from it is not a pleasure in the reproduction of natural or human life. The disgust with the trivial and accidental characteristics of living shapes, the searching after an austerity, a *perfection* and rigidity which vital things can never have, lead here to the use of forms which can almost be called geometrical. Man is subordinate to certain absolute values; there is no delight in the human form, leading to its *natural* reproduction; it is always distorted to fit into the more abstract forms which convey an intense religious emotion. These two arts thus correspond exactly to the thought of their respective periods. Byzantine art to the ideology which looks on man and all existing things as imperfect and sinful in comparison with certain abstract values and *perfections*. The other art corresponds to the humanist ideology, which looks on man and life as good, and which is thus in a relation of harmony with existence.

It is interesting that just before this passage was a

9

reference to Max Weber and the other economists who connect the rise of usury and of capitalism with the decline of the religious spirit: yet another reason in some quarters for condemning the Renaissance as a whole.

Luckily, we do not have to choose between these two crude extremes I have been presenting. We are free to compromise: to agree with Miss Sichel about the magnificence of Michelangelo's Adam and yet to refuse to pit him so starkly against medieval asceticism; to admire Byzantine mosaics with Hulme and yet to think his scorn of Renaissance art to be a false and bigoted simplification. For when you come to think of it coolly, Hulme's simplification is indeed ridiculous. He writes as if the whole point of Renaissance art was its joy in living forms, as if the abstract and formal side did not exist for it. If anything is obvious about Renaissance art, it is that it used principles of composition at once different from the medieval and yet having nothing to do with any joy or lack of joy in living forms. Further, the amount of this joy will vary enormously from one artist to another. But even when it is very great, as in Michelangelo or Titian, it can coexist with an equally great if not greater delight in the abstractions of pure form. In some pictures, for example the large allegories of Paul Veronese, joy in the human body hardly exists compared with the vastly preponderant interest in the sheer composition: the spectator has to force himself into any curiosity about the subject treated or the human attributes of the figures represented. But this is a digression and I return to my point that we are free to compromise; and for such a compromise there is now very strong authority. One of the finest achievements of modern scholarship (and American scholars have been prominent in it) has been to link up the medieval and Elizabethan backgrounds, to follow up the trends of thought from the periods of Mont-Saint-Michel and Chartres and to see what became of them in the epoch of the new learning and the reformed religion. And the result has been twofold: first, to find that the beginnings of the Renaissance spirit go back right into the authentic Middle Ages; and secondly, that the Middle Ages did not end with either a bang or a whimper in the fifteenth or early sixteenth century, but that they continued well into the seventeenth century side by side with the rise of the scientific spirit. Let me illustrate.

As far back as 1872, Walter Pater in an essay which became the second one in the *Renaissance* described and confirmed the notion, already formulated by French scholars, of a kind of pre-renaissance in France at the end of the twelfth and beginning of the thirteenth centuries. It flowered above all in the sculpture of Chartres and the windows of Le Mans, works which look forward "thus healing that rupture between the middle age and the Renaissance

11

which has so often been exaggerated." But it had other flowerings too, and I quote from Pater's account of them:

Here and there, under rare and happy conditions, in pointed architecture, in the doctrines of romantic love, in the poetry of Provence, the rude strength of the middle ages turns to sweetness; and the taste for sweetness generated there becomes the seed of the classical revival in it, prompting it constantly to seek after the springs of perfect sweetness in the Hellenic world. And coming after a long period in which this instinct had been crushed, that true "dark age," in which so many sources of intellectual and imaginative enjoyment had actually disappeared, this outbreak is rightly called a Renaissance, a revival.

Pater, of course, does to this medieval outbreak what the nineteenth-century critics did to eighteenth-century poetry, namely detach from that age whatever they found congenial and, robbing that age of all credit, praise the works for being precursors of a better time. Thus Thomson's *Castle of Indolence* was separated from its true context of the elegant Spenserian burlesque, so typically Augustan, and made, on account of certain highly musical and picturesque stanzas, to foretell the coming of a greater poet, Keats. But that is better than condemning the whole age. W. P. Ker went much farther than Pater and postulated a different break altogether. This was in the twelfth century, when the round romanesque arch was replaced by the pointed Gothic, and

12

the starkness of the Teutonic epic tradition gave way to the sophistication of the romance and the complexities of medieval philosophy. The true dawn of humanism was in the twelfth century. Here is Ker's statement, published as far back as 1896 in *Epic and Romance*, one of the most prophetic made by an academic critic:

The change of fashion in the twelfth century is as momentous and far-reaching in its consequences as that to which the name " Renaissance " is generally appropriated. The later Renaissance, indeed, in what concerns imaginative literature, makes no such abrupt and sudden change of fashion as was made in the twelfth century. The poetry and romance of the Renaissance follow naturally upon the literature of the Midddle Ages; for the very good reason that it was the Middle Ages which began, even in their dark beginnings, the modern study of the humanities, and in the twelfth century made a remarkable and determined effort to secure the inheritance of ancient poetry for the advantage of the new tongues and their new forms of verse. There is no such line of diversion between Ariosto and Chrestien of Troyes as there is between Chrestien and the primitive epic.

I am not concerned with the many detailed connections or instances of gradual transitions between the two epochs that have been perceived since Ker published *Epic and Romance* in 1896, but I will give in passing a single instance of the kind of thing that has been happening, to the great enlightenment of

13

our understanding. It comes from a part of ecclesiastical activity, the sermon.

If you had asked our hypothetical Victorian what constituted the main characteristics of medieval and reformed religious practice respectively, he would have given ritual to the first and the sermon to the second. What has happened since? Owst has shown us the strength and extent of medieval preaching. Haller has seen that this tradition was taken over by the Puritan preachers in the reign of Elizabeth, so that there is no break between the Middle Ages and the pulpit's great age in the seventeenth century. Christopher Dawson has remarked of Langland, who uses sermon material freely, " that his spiritual successors are to be found not in the Catholic Church, nor even in the Church of England, but among the Puritans and the rebels, with Fox and Bunyan and Whitfield and Blake." Not that we should be surprised. Had we not known with our intellects that Bunyan's *Pilgrim's Progress* was in the pure tradition of the medieval allegory of the *pélerinage de l'âme humaine*? And should not our imaginations have assured us that this could be no isolated phenomenon?

To this conviction that there was no break between the medieval and Renaissance worlds I made a minor contribution in my *Elizabethan World Picture*. In that book I chose to dwell on the similarities between the epochs; and there is always the danger

14

of making too much of them. It is partly on account of this danger that here I shall dwell more on the differences. Or let me put it in this way. Granted there is no abrupt rift between medieval and Renaissance, it is yet true that in the later period certain trends, going back if you will to the twelfth century, were greatly speeded up and developed so as to present an impression of novelty.

My plan here is to examine in a general way three types of opinion or feeling traditionally attached to the Renaissance and then in subsequent chapters to apply my findings to the three types of literature already mentioned: the lyric, literary criticism, and the epic.

Laurie Magnus, whose general sketch of European literature in the age of romance was published in 1918, illustrated the supposed humanist, anti-ascetic doctrine of the Renaissance, which Miss Sichel found in Michelangelo's Adam, from a passage in *Hamlet*. He thought that the whole philosophy of the Renaissance was contained in Hamlet's perception:

What a piece of work is a man! How noble in reason, how infinite in faculty, in form and moving how express and admirable, in action how like an angel, in apprehension how like a god! the beauty of the world, the paragon of animals!

Others before him had thought the same; and it had

15

been common to quote Sophocles's famous chorus on man in the *Antigone* to show that Shakespeare was a true son of the Renaissance in reproducing a classical statement. Sophocles wrote:

Wonders are many and none is more wonderful than man; the power that crosses the white sea, driven by the stormy south-wind, making a path under surges that threaten to engulf him; and Earth, the eldest of the gods, the immortal, the unwearied, doth he wear, turning the soil with the offspring of horses, as the ploughs go to and fro from year to year. . . . And speech and wind-swift thought, and all the moods that mould a state, hath he taught himself; and how to flee the arrows of frost, when it is hard lodging under the clear sky, and the arrows of the rushing rain; yea, he hath resource for all.

To Magnus's opinion it can be retorted that Hamlet is far from asserting the unmixed dignity of man against the asceticisms of medieval misanthropy. Actually he is being very medieval and is simply quoting the orthodox encomia of what man, because created in God's image, ideally was. Nor do you need to go to Sophocles for a comparison. The theologians had been talking like that for centuries. Here is an example from as far back as the fourth century A.D.:

No eloquence may worthily publish forth the manifold pre-eminences and advantages which are bestowed on man. He passes over the vast seas; he ranges about the wide heavens by his contemplation and conceives the motions

16

and magnitudes of the stars. . . . He is learned in every science and skilful in artificial workings. He talks with angels, yea with God himself. He has all creatures within his dominion.

Further, Hamlet has a very lively picture of another conception of man which in traditional thought balanced the picture just given: that of man depraved by sin.

I am very proud, revengeful, ambitious, with more offences at my beck than I have thought to put them in, imagination to give them shape, or time to act them in. What should such fellows as I do crawling between earth and heaven? We are arrant knaves, all.

That Hamlet is mixing much irony with his self-condemnation does not make his words any less in the tradition of medieval orthodoxy.

And yet it would not be right to leave the matter there. Let us take a second and equally famous passage of Shakespeare and seek a comparison with the Middle Ages. At the end of *Julius Caesar*, Antony says of Brutus:

> *This was the noblest Roman of them all,*
> *All the conspirators save only he*
> *Did that they did in envy of great Caesar:*
> *He only, in a general honest thought*
> *And common good of all, made one of them.*
> *His life was gentle, and the elements*
> *So mix'd in him that Nature might stand up*
> *And say to all the world " This was a man."*

17

There is far less sense here of human depravity than in *Hamlet*; and it makes little difference to say, as can be said, that you would not expect it in the context of a Roman play. The point is that Shakespeare can be at ease in such a context in a new way. He can attribute more sheer merit to Brutus simply for being a fine specimen of a man than was possible in the Middle Ages. Let me take an extreme contrast, three verses from the *Dies Irae*, one of the grandest medieval hymns, dating probably from the thirteenth century:

> *Dies irae, dies illa*
> *Solvet saeclum in favilla*
> *Teste David cum Sibylla.*
> (" *Day of wrath, that day when the world*
> *shall fall into ashes, witness David and*
> *the Sibyl.*")

> *Quantus tremor est futurus,*
> *Quando iudex est venturus,*
> *Cuncta stricte discussurus!*
> (" *How great a trembling will there be,*
> *when the judge shall come, to examine*
> *closely all our deeds.*")

> *Quid sum miser tunc dicturus,*
> *Quem patronum rogaturus,*
> *Cum vix iustus sit securus?*
> (" *What shall I, wretch, say then, what*
> *protector shall I invoke, when even a*
> *good man shall scarcely be safe?* ")

18

You see the negation of humanism, of any human virtue in man's own right, especially in the last line. Mankind is lost and wicked; and even a good man (like Brutus) is in a precarious position. Or take Malory's Launcelot and his behavior at the healing of Sir Urry. It had been brought about by enchantment that Sir Urry " should never be whole until the best knight of the world had searched his wounds." Many knights try. Launcelot in his modesty is terribly reluctant to try where others have failed. But Arthur commanded him.

And then Sir Launcelot prayed Sir Urry to let him see his head; and then, devoutly kneeling, he ransacked the three wounds that they bled a little; and forthwith all the wounds fair healed and seemed as they had been whole a seven year. And in like wise he searched his body of other three wounds and they healed in like wise. And then the last of all he searched his hand and anon it fair healed. Then King Arthur and all the kings and knights kneeled down and gave thankings and loving unto God and unto his blessed Mother. And ever Sir Launcelot wept, as he had been a child that had been beaten.

To see in these tears, as Vinaver does (and let nothing I say lessen my sense of admiration for his great edition of Malory), a foreboding of a tragic reversal of fortune is surely to misinterpret grossly. Launcelot's tears are for the wretched pettiness of human glory in the shadow of God's changeless world.

Such tears have little place in the world of Shakespeare's Brutus.

Once again we must be wary and not suppose that everybody would have approved of Shakespeare's arrogating so much to his Brutus. The Calvinists would certainly not have done so but would have felt themselves in closer sympathy with the *Dies Irae*. This is Calvin on the nature of man:

The mind of man is so entirely alienated from the righteousness of God that he cannot conceive, desire, or design anything but what is wicked, distorted, impure, and iniquitous; that his heart is so thoroughly envenomed by sin, that it can breathe out nothing but corruption and rottenness; that if some men occasionally make a show of goodness, their mind is ever interwoven with hypocrisy and deceit, their soul inwardly bound with the fetters of wickedness.

But I am speaking of England not Scotland; and in England the Calvinists were a small, though vigorous, minority.

It is, then, on a balance no fiction that the conception of man's position changed from the Middle Ages to the Renaissance. The Elizabethan conception was neither that of the *Dies Irae* nor of another hymn: the one shouted by Swinburne into the shocked ears of the Victorian middle classes:

Glory to Man in the highest! for Man is the master of things.

20

It was aware of both these incompatibles and to its glory succeeded in combining a measure of each.

A second commonplace concerning the Renaissance is that there arose a new freedom of speculation. I do not use the word in its financial sense, though it is widely held that what we associate with the city of London and Wall Street was rooted in the Renaissance. Speculation here refers to ideas on the nature of man and of the universe. Now whether the commonplace is true depends on what you mean by it. If you mean that there was little speculation in the Middle Ages and then there came a sudden change and there was a great deal in the Renaissance, you would be fantastically wrong. There was a very great deal of speculation in the Middle Ages, but it was mainly within certain defined areas. The historians of science tell us of the amount of speculative ingenuity employed by the medieval astronomers in seeking to reconcile the two authoritative but in many ways differing systems of Aristotle and Ptolemy. Dante had a highly speculative mind, and yet one is very conscious of the limits in which he worked. It is also possible to exaggerate that daring spirit of speculation attributed to certain Elizabethans. The author usually pointed to is Marlowe; and among illustrations from him the lines from *Tamburlaine* about infinite knowledge.

> *Nature, that fram'd us of four elements,*
> *Warring within our breasts for regiment,*

21

Doth teach us all to have aspiring minds.
Our souls, whose faculties can comprehend
The wondrous architecture of the world
And measure every wand'ring planet's course,
Still climbing after knowledge infinite
And always moving as the restless spheres,
Wills us to wear ourselves and never rest,
Until we reach the ripest fruit of all,
That perfect bliss and sole felicity,
The sweet fruition of an earthly crown.

This passage and Faustus's search for experience are taken to indicate a spirit of exultation that the fruit of the tree of knowledge is no longer forbidden—or, if it is forbidden, so much the more exciting—

For lust of knowing what should not be known
We make the Golden Journey to Samarcand.

But there is still much medievalism in Marlowe. The theme of dangerous or forbidden knowledge is just as much the property of the Middle Ages as of James Elroy Flecker. And the defiant spirit of Tamburlaine is as closely allied to the ordinary manifestations of the first of the seven deadly sins as to a new spirit of free speculation. So we must beware here, as elsewhere, of separating the Middle Ages and Renaissance too sharply.

Yet, if you take not so much this or that manifestation but the prevailing climate, there was a true change. And it amounted to this: that by the Elizabethan age men had *options* of free and novel speculations denied to the Middle Ages. Fewer people may have used these options than has been often imagined, but their existence meant a great deal. Montaigne had dared to question the rigidity of the boundaries separating the different orders of creation; in his *Apology for Raimond Sebond* he wrote:

With this same vanity of imagination man makes himself the equal of God, assumes to himself divine qualities, selects and separates himself from among the multitude of other creatures, carves out their shares to each of his fellows and comrades, the animals, and allots to them their portion of faculties and powers according as it seems good to him. How can he know, by the force of his understanding, the secret internal motions of the animals? By what comparison between them and himself does he suppose them to be as stupid as he thinks? When I play with my cat, who knows but she regards me more as a plaything than I do her? We amuse each other with our respective monkey-tricks; if I have my moments for beginning and refusing, so she has hers.

Now to put men and animals on such an equality as this was to confound the laws of the Vast Chain of Being, and to cast doubts on the absolute dominion over animals which God had granted Adam at the time of creation.

Well, such speculative subversiveness did not prevent Montaigne's essays being translated into

English and widely read. And even if England had to wait until well after Bacon for the spirit of speculation to become dominant, it had become possible before he himself had reached maturity.

We now turn to the third type of feeling associated with the Renaissance. As one of the most popular and influential books of that age was Castiglioni's *Courtier*, so Spenser made Courtesy one of the ethical virtues forming subjects of the books of the *Fairy Queen*. Now the typically Elizabethan virtue of Courtesy is plainly inherited from the medieval ideal of Chivalry. Does the one extend and modify the other, or has a new principle entered in? That is an unfair form of question, because to both alternatives the answer should be yes. Both principles are alike in being grounded on religion and in postulating certain high standards; and yet an element, important in the history of civilization, has entered into the Elizabethan virtue. Now the medieval code was founded on an abstract ideal. A well-bred man was expected to behave in a certain way to a well-bred woman, whether she were Margaret or Mary or Elizabeth, and whether or not Margaret or Mary or Elizabeth liked it. It may seem that to posit such abstraction is to go against the most famous of all English descriptions of knighthood, those of the Knight and Squire in the Prologue to the *Canterbury Tales*. Surely the Knight with his tunic spotted by his coat-of-mail, and the Squire with his locks

curled " as they were leyd in presse " and his modest
demeanor when he carved before his father are realistic figures, remote from abstraction. I think not:
for however vividly the two are circumstantiated—
and Chaucer here writes at the height of his powers
—the figures themselves are ideal. Look carefully at
their parts and their achievements, and you will see
that they are free from the accidents of real life. In
his " mortal battles " the Knight *never* failed to kill
his foe:

> *He nevere yet no vileyne ne sayde*
> *In al his lyf unto no maner wight.*

Surely no human being has ever really achieved that
degree of self-restraint. And the Squire, as lover,
succeeded in cutting out all sleep (like the nightingale), not because mortal lovers can really succeed
but because as an ideal they should be imagined to do
so. And so, when Chaucer calls his Knight's bearing
" as meeke as is a mayde " he is picturing him as
conforming to an *ideal* of chivalry; and the question
whether the folk on whom he practised his meekness
liked or disliked it simply does not arise.

This mention of Chaucer prompts me to inter-
rupt my present argument to deal with a general
principle for a few minutes. The principle is this:
the imperative need, in any comparative discussion
of epochs, first to decide what the norm of an epoch
is and then not to vary the grounds of your decision

from epoch to epoch. If in one epoch you choose for your norm the pioneer spirits and the advance guard of thought, and in another the natural conservatism of the majority, you will achieve the most fantastic results, even if your separate assessments are perfectly correct. Scholars do not usually go on quite like that, but if they have an idea they are very anxious to prove true they may unconsciously commit such a distortion. Anyhow it is essential that writers on movements of thought should make it clear where they fix their norm; and for myself I favor a middle position, one that is shared neither by the pioneers nor by the diehards. You want to discover the commonplaces, the unargued presuppositions, that animate the middle type of thinking men at any one time. If you anthologise the most startling thoughts of the most advanced thinkers, you will find yourself very far from that position.

I have just cited Chaucer's Knight and Squire as typically medieval figures, but I did not mean to suggest that you can always use Chaucer in that way. It is, of course, the fashion now to see Chaucer thus. C. S. Lewis has written excellently to prove how medieval are the things Chaucer takes for granted in *Troylus and Criseyde*; and such demonstrations are often taken to have deflated for good the claims for Chaucer's going beyond his age made, for instance, by Lounsbury and Mackail. I do not believe they have done anything of the sort. Even

26

if in *Troylus and Criseyde* Chaucer started from medieval assumptions he did end, among other things, in creating the first psychological novel in English.

Or take another poem of Chaucer's, *The House of Fame*, and you will find in it a passage that, for all its medieval apparatus, ends by whisking you right away from any medieval setting. The passage occurs in the third book, and it describes the different companies of folk who come to the House of Fame to inquire about, or agitate for, their reputation. First comes a company of virtuous people who would like their proper recompense; and Fame sends them packing with the statement that they will acquire no fame, either good or bad. Then she sends for Aeolus to come with his two trumpets: the golden one to blow praise abroad, the black one slander. A second company of the same sort as the first arrives; and though they have done well in life, Fame condemns them to be slandered. With the third company of the same sort, she does the opposite and grants them more reputation than they merit. Then, in abrupt contrast, comes a fourth company, and a very small one. They too have done well in life, but fame does not interest them: they did as they did " for bounty." They are in fact the small company of the disinterested, who do good for good's sake and not for any reward. And Fame is quite content that they should pass unknown. Next come a second company of those who do not want fame: they are those who did good for the love of God and contemplation. And though presumably they have their eye on fame in another life, Fame capriciously insists on their having it in this. The next two companies are of those who want fame though they have done nothing to deserve it; and Fame grants the request of one and refuses that of the other. Finally she refuses fame to the ordinary criminals, but grants it to the psychological perverts who do bad deeds for the sole reason of calling attention to themselves. It is an astonishing survey of human types (the inclusion of the small company of the disinterested being the most astonishing single item) and of the vagaries of chance in this world: and, as we read it, the Middle Ages, or any age, become irrelevant; we are in a timeless realm of basic human nature.

Let me add one other example, from outside English literature. In the passage praising country life at the end of the second book of the *Georgics*, Virgil gives certain reasons why a man may be glad not to live in a great city. One of these is that he is not racked with fruitless pity for the sufferings of the poor. Now this is a most surprising sentiment, for the Romans were not greatly given to pity. But our comment should be not that Virgil here showed himself to be humanitarian in a " modern " way but that he was an exceptional man, a man of universal sympathies, who through them raised himself above the norm of his age and joined the choice company of those who in other ages succeeded in doing the same. How mistaken, too, to take these passages in Chaucer and Virgil or analogous passages in any author of the first rank as evidence of ways of thinking in the periods where these passages belong. And what an ironic message such passages convey to the research student with his set theme and his card-index, eager for grist to his mill, for the extracts which, conviently removed from their context, will help him to complete the piece of work that authority, before which the humble individual is powerless, ordains him to undertake if he is to earn a living as a university teacher.

These remarks on Chaucer should serve to demonstrate that if a scholar intends to use an author to illustrate the current opinions of his age he should, before committing himself, decide if that author is in fact representative. Further, if an author, found on the whole to be thus representative, is a great and original spirit, the scholar may have to decide whether any portions of his work go beyond his age in such a way as to cease to be representative. Take the period of the Romantic Revival. Wordsworth, Shelley, and Keats are too great innovators to be the most centrally representative. Cowper, greatly read, is a little too old-fashioned. Crabbe for the earlier portion, Scott and Byron for the later, are better representatives than any of

29

these. And here are two small pieces of evidence. It was from Crabbe that " Monk " Lewis took his title-quotation in 1808 for his *Romantic Tales*. In the *Spirit of the Age* (1825), Hazlitt wrote that Scott and Byron would get the most votes for the place of chief geniuses of their age. But Scott and Byron were in some ways highly original writers, and we should not accept all they have to say as necessarily voicing the thoughts and feelings of their fellows. To revert to the Middle Ages, it is probable that Gower makes a safer representative of his period than, as a whole, Chaucer does. And with this remark I may get back to the topic of Courtesy.

Now into the idea of Courtesy there entered the element of human consideration that was lacking in the medieval ideal of the knight, and, as the years went on, it grew in importance at the expense of the rigid scheme in which it first germinated. Not that the element was absent from medieval literature, only it is felt to be subordinate. Henryson was a poet naturally gifted with a very sensitive human sympathy; and that sympathy takes exquisite form in the pity which he bestows on his Cresseid in the *Testament of Cresseid*. But such pity is felt *within* the great prevailing setting of orthodox theology. Cresseid acts according to the classic scheme of orthodox fall and salvation.* She falls into two of

* See my *Five Poems: 1470–1870* for a development of this contention.

30

the deadly sins: lechery and pride. She undergoes a dreadful punishment, but to her own good. For a time her pride holds, but finally the spectacle of Troilus's fidelity and generosity melts it and she takes all blame for her misfortunes on herself. And she dies a repentant sinner. Nevertheless, as is only to be expected, there are hints in medieval writers of a new disposition. For instance, into some of Lydgate's expostulations with Guido delle Colonne, his original in the *Troy Book*, on Guido's bitter condemnation of women, the element of human consideration has entered. It was in the early Tudor age that the element came into sufficient prominence to be able to change the chivalric into the courtly ideal. And the men who chiefly promoted it were Erasmus and More. R. W. Chambers has exploded the fiction that *Utopia* was a pure work of the Renaissance and a violent break with the Middle Ages. Its doctrine turns out to be well rooted in the immediate past. But this does not prevent the tone of the book being new. In spite of his personal asceticisms More showed a new faculty of sympathy, of entering imaginatively in the other person's place. It is a faculty he showed also in his treatment of the unfortunate Jane Shore, mistress of Edward IV, in his *History of Richard III*.

As a contrast to the implications of Chaucer's Knight and Squire, let us take those of a famous place in literature: Fulke Greville's description of the death of Philip Sidney, the man who was Spenser's model of Courtesy for the sixth book of the *Fairy Queen*. It is a long description containing much more than the episode in it that has made it famous. I will quote that episode and one other passage. Referring to an unexpected stand by the enemy before the walls of Zutphen, Greville wrote as follows:

Howsoever, by this stand, an unfortunate hand out of those forespoken trenches brake the bone of Sir Philip's thigh with a musket-shot. The horse he rode upon was rather furiously choleric than bravely proud and so forced him to forsake the field, but not his back as the noblest and fittest bier to carry a martial commander to his grave. In which sad progress, passing along by the rest of the army, where his uncle the General was, and being thirsty with excess of bleeding, he called for drink, which was presently brought him. But as he was putting the bottle to his mouth, he saw a poor soldier carried along, who had eaten his last at the same feast, ghastly casting up his eyes at the bottle. Which Sir Philip perceiving, took it from his head before he drank and delivered it to the poor man with these words: " Thy necessity is yet greater than mine." And when he had pledged this poor soldier he was presently carried to Arnheim.

Such fine acts are performed by fine people in all ages but they get differently explained. In the Middle Ages the act would have been one of saintliness, the giving of a scriptural cup of cold water, and saintly with little or no regard to the degree in which the common soldier wanted the drink. The act's essential reference would have been to an abstract ideal of conduct. But with Sidney the personal consideration entered; and it was because the soldier's thirst was so great that he got the drink. Sidney acted thus through putting himself in the other man's place. When Sidney found himself in the hands of the surgeons, he told them to let no pain he suffered hinder them in the exercise of their art. And part of his motive was a care for their own medical practice and reputation—I quote Greville's words:

When they began to dress his wounds, he both by way of charge and advice told them that while his strength was yet entire, his body free from fever, and his mind able to endure, they might freely use their art: cut and search to the bottom. For besides his hope of health, he would make this farther profit of the pains which he must suffer that they should bear witness they had indeed a sensible natured man under their hands, yet one to whom a stronger Spirit had given power above himself, either to do or suffer. But if they should now neglect their art and renew torments in the declination of nature, their ignorance or over-tenderness would prove a kind of tyranny to their friend and consequently a blemish to their reverend science.

Such a consideration for others may even appear exaggerated; but at least it is sharply contrasted with the ways of thought governing medieval literature.

I have described three general ways in which the English sixteenth century, the age of the English Renaissance, differed from the English Middle Ages; and the trend of each way was to give an enlarged scope to the human spirit as such. In some ways, at least, the old commonplace about human emancipation turns out not to lack all support. In subsequent sections we shall inquire into a similar development in three literary forms.

II

The Lyric

WALTER PATER in the essay mentioned above chose the poetry of Provence as one of the constituents of that "Renaissance within the limits of the middle age itself." He was right to speak of that poetry in terms of a new birth, but wrong to suggest that this early Renaissance was islanded, a separate anticipatory outburst rather than the beginning of the whole evolution; for the Provençal lyric, travelling northwards to the heart of Gothic France, helped to establish a lyric tradition in England whose expiring notes were those cavalier songs of the age of Charles II which carry on so plainly the tradition from before the Commonwealth. It is just because of this continuity that the lyric offers so convenient a means of answering our question whether the English Renaissance was fact or fiction.

In the whole of the great English lyrical tradition from the thirteenth to the seventeenth centuries there is a blend of folk and of courtly elements; that is one of its main charms; but it must not be supposed that this folk element continued unaltered from an earlier age. On the contrary, within it there occurred a fundamental change, corresponding perhaps to the great changes already mentioned from primitive epic to romance and from round to pointed arch. However much of folk *rhythm* may have penetrated into the mass of the English lyric, the old folk *themes* of the love lyric underwent a fundamental change. In the folk tradition it is the woman who makes the advances; in the new lyric tradition it is the man, according to the new courtly convention imported from the Troubadours. Here are verses from an English folk song which, in spite of the mention of guns, must in its original form go back far before their invention:

> *If all these young men were as hares on the*
> *mountain,*
> *Then all those pretty maidens will get guns,*
> *go a-huntin'.*
>
> *If all these young men were as rushes a-*
> *growin',*
> *Then all those pretty maidens will get scythes,*
> *go a-mowin'.*
>
> *If all these young men were as ducks in the*
> *water,*
> *Then all those pretty maidens will soon*
> *follow a'ter.*

36

It is remarkable that the polite tradition was dominant till the Russian novelists and *Man and Superman*, though Jane Austen shows herself perfectly unprejudiced in the matter. Catherine Morland in *Northanger Abbey*, though a young woman of high propriety, does in fact, though not in appearance, take the initiative. Anyhow, the polite tradition was established so early and so thoroughly that, when later the fashion for Petrarch arose with his eternal themes of the adoring lover and flinty-hearted mistress, it implied no innovation but merely that an earlier convention was intensified and stylized. I shall not seek in Petrarch for the signs of a true Renaissance in the English lyric.

Nor can one profitably seek them in any technical improvement. It is useless to argue that the English medieval lyric was crude and primitive while the Renaissance English lyric was elegant and professional, or that the cadences of the medieval lyric were remote from music compared with the wonderful wedding of words and tune to be found in Campion or other artists of the Elizabethan songbooks. On the contrary, enough secular lyrics have survived from the thirteenth century in England (and Carleton Brown thinks that far more would have survived if the copyists had not been monks and hence prejudiced against them) to show that the art was at its height in that age. Many of the best come from a single manuscript, sometimes known as Harley 2253 and sometimes the Leominster manuscript from its origin in a priory there. They are widely known, several of them, as some of the first lyrics in the *Oxford Book of English Verse*. I mean, among others, the songs beginning " Betwene Mersh and Averil," " Lenten is come with love to toune," " When the nyhtegale singes," and " Nou shrinketh rose ant lylie flour." These lyrics are completely competent and sure of themselves : there is nothing in the least amateurish about them. Also, they suggest by a certain yieldingness of movement the need of a musical setting; and this, combined with their elegance and refinement, presents that union of folk and courtly elements that has been the glory of this great lyric movement. Just so, the themes of the developed English Renaissance lyric may be dominated by the Petrarchian fashion, but the music of " Forget not yet the tried intent " (Wyatt), " Fear no more the heat of the sun " (Shakespeare), " Follow your saint, follow with accents sweet " (Campion) is native and goes back to the medieval tradition with its reinforcing infusion of the folk element. But it is time to illustrate. For sheer poetic competence take the first verse of " Winter wakeneth."

> *Winter wakeneth all my care,*
> *Now these leaves waxeth bare;*
> *Oft I sike and mourne sare*
> > *When it cometh in my thought*
> > *Of this world's joy, how it go'th all to nought.*

Technically, the way sound echoes sense here is per-
fect, while the last line with its reluctant rhythm and
its eight monosyllables is triumphant. The author
has nothing to learn. For the suggestion of the
musical beat and a brilliant change of rhythm play-
ing into the hand of the musical composer, take the
last verse of the Alison poem. I quote the second and
last verses, first giving a translation:

Her hair is very beautiful in color, her brow dark and
her eye black. She smiled at me with a delightful expression. She has a small and elegant waist. If she refuses to
take me for her partner, I shall soon quit living and be
fated to fall down as dead. (*Refrain*): I have got hold
of a lucky lot; I think it has been sent me from heaven.
My love is diverted from all women and lights on Alison.

I am kept from sleeping through my wooing, weary as
water in a weir. I have worried grievously lest anyone
should deprive me of my mate. It is better to endure hard
things for a while than to mourn for ever. Gainliest in
your dress, listen to my song. (*Refrain as before.*)

> *On heu hire her is fayr ynoh,*
> *Hire browe broune, hire eye blake.*
> *With lossum chere he on me loh;*
> *With middel smal and wel y-make.*
> *Bote he me wille to hire take*
> *For to buen hire owen make,*
> *Longe to lyven ichulle forsake*
> *Ant feye fallen adoun.*

An hendy hap ichabbe yhent;
Ichot from hevene it is me sent.
From alle wymmen mi love is lent
Ant lyht on Alysoun.

Icham for wowing all forwake,
Wery so water in wore.
Lest eny reve me my make
Ichabbe y-yerned yore.
Betere is tholien whyle sore,
Then mournen evermore.
Geynest under gore,
Herkne to my roun.

An hendy hap ichabbe yhent;
Ichot from hevene it is me sent.
From alle wymmen mi love is lent
Ant lyht on Alysoun.

The sudden change to the joyful and emphatic beat
of " Geynest under gore " from the drawn-out melancholy of " Betere is tholien whyle sore, Then
mournen evermore " is typical of what the Elizabethan song-writers could do three centuries later.

Or take the mysterious little lyric about the maid
who lay out seven nights on the moor, with the prim-
rose and the violet for her food, with cold water
from the spring for her drink, and the red rose and
the lily for her bed. It is scribbled with eleven other
pieces and fragments (two of them in French) on
the leaf of a manuscript in the Bodleian Library.
W. Heuser first published them in the thirtieth

volume of *Anglia*, and Kenneth Sisam made the *Maid of the Moor* known by including it in his anthology of fourteenth century verse and prose. Miss Sitwell, with her wonderfully fine ear for poetic melody, has commented on it in her *Poet's Notebook*. In substance the lyric is of the most fragile, but in accomplishment—call it technical accomplishment—it is perfection. Here it is with the slight but certain restorations made by Sisam.

> *Maiden in the mor lay,*
> *In the mor lay,*
> *Sevenyst fulle, sevennist fulle,*
> *Maiden in the mor lay,*
> *In the mor lay,*
> *Sevenistes fulle ant a day.*
>
> *Welle was hire mete:*
> *Wat was hire mete?*
> *The primerole ant the—*
> *The primerole ant the—*
> *Welle was hire mete;*
> *Wat was hire mete?*
> *The primerole ant the violet.*
>
> *Welle was hire dryng:*
> *Wat was hire dryng?*
> *The chelde water of the welle-spring.*
>
> *Welle was hire bour:*
> *Wat was hire bour?*
> *The rede rose an te lilie flour.*

If I may stray a little from my immediate subject, I should like to express my lively curiosity about who the maiden on the moor was. Can she be identified, or is the poem a piece of airy fantasy, hovering like Mahomet's coffin between heaven and earth? I have consulted two medievalists without result; neither editor considers annotation necessary. The only help I have met is in the fifteenth passus of *Piers Plowman* (B-text), where the ascetic lives of various saints are recounted: Anthony, Egidius, Paul the Hermit, and St. Peter. And then come the lines:

> *And also Marie Magdeleyne by mores lyved and*
> *dewes*
> *Ac moste thorw devocioun and mynde of God*
> *Almighty.*

If Mary Magdalene lived " by moors and dews," may not the maiden who lay in the moor be another saint of similar habits? It is true that all the other poems on the sheet of the manuscript are secular, but the same minstrel could have sung both secular and sacred songs.

Carleton Brown notes that in the thirteenth century, much more than in the fourteenth, lyrics were composed to be sung: the later century was more the age of the literary as against the musical lyric. The difference between these types is more easily felt than described. If we compare the Alison song with Dr. Johnson's " Long expected one-and-twenty " or

Felicia Hemans's " The boy stood on the burning deck," that difference would be very apparent. But it is worth mentioning two ways in which a lyric can prove itself a song, something requiring music. The first way is for the words as it were to demand music, to cry aloud for it, to insist. It is the way of

> *Adam lay i-bounden*
> *Bounden in a bond*

or

> *Follow your saint, follow with accents sweet.*

The second way is the coy one, not that of insisting on or pursuing the music. It works through weakness, through incompleteness, through winning the support of music, because music knows that a collapse is threatened. Some of the most beautiful lyrics work that way:

> *I saw a fair maiden*
> *Sitten and sing,*
> *She lulled a litel child*
> *A sweet lording,*
>
> *That eche lord is that*
> *That made alle thing;*
> *Of alle lordes he is lord*
> *Of alle kinges king.*

There is hardly any substance here, and yet there is the sense of an exquisite completeness when music has made up the deficiencies.

Certainly, " Adam lay i-bounden," and " I saw a fair maiden " belong to the fifteenth century and show that the musical lyric, less prominent in the fourteenth, blossomed again in the later carols. There was no break in the tradition. Other fifteenth century lyrics show something else: the influence of the religious drama. I will quote some stanzas in illustration, and partly because, though dramatic, they are so in a way very different from Wyatt (my next topic), whose sense of drama is something new and unmedieval. They come from a dramatic monologue of Christ speaking from the cross, and it is just possible that Skelton is the author:

> *Woefully arrayed,*
> *My blood, man,*
> *For thee ran:*
> *It may not be nayed;*
> *My body blue and wan,*
> *Woefully arrayed.*

> *Behold me, I pray thee, with all thy whole reason,*
> *And be not so hard-hearted, and for this encheason,*
> *Sith I for thy soul's sake was slain in good season,*
> *Beguiled and betrayed by Judas' false treason;*
> *Unkindly entreated,*
> *With sharp cord sore fretted,*
> *The Jewes me threated;*
> *They mowed, they grinned, they scorned me,*
> *Condemned to death, as thou mayest see;*
> *Woefully arrayed.*

Thus naked am I nailed, O man, for they sake!
I love thee, then love me; why sleepest thou? awake!
Remember my tender heart-root for thee brake;
With paines my veines constrained to crake;
>   *Thus tugged to and fro,*
>   *Thus wrapped all in wo,*
>   *Whereas ne'er man was so*
>   *Entreated thus in most cruel wise;*
>   *Was like a lamb offered for sacrifice,*
>   *Woefully arrayed.*

This is a powerful piece of writing, overwhelmingly full of detail, sharply opposed to the refinement and fragility of the carols. In its accumulation of violent physical detals it recalls contemporary Teutonic paintings of the Crucifixion. And if the comparison I shall draw between this type of lyric and Wyatt is to be made vivid, please remember the Teutonic and Italian strains in the religious pictures of the Netherlands, and especially of Flanders, in the late fifteenth and early sixteenth centuries.

In the sixteenth century the secular lyric predominates; music and song have become the fashionable accomplishments of the courtier. I will quote one lyric, dating from very early in the century, to establish a second point of contrast with Wyatt.

>   *By a bank as I lay,*
>   *Musing myself alone, hey ho!*
>   *A birdes voice*
>   *Did me rejoice,*

Singing before the day;
And me thought in her lay
She said, winter was past, hey ho!
Then dyry come dawn, dyry come dyry, come dyry!
Come dyry, come dyry, come dawn, hey ho!

The master of music,
The lusty nightingale, hey ho!
Full merrily
And secretly
She singeth in the thick;
And under her breast a prick,
To keep her fro sleep, hey ho!

Awake, therefore, young men,
All ye that lovers be, hey ho!
This month of May,
So fresh, so gay,
So fair be fields on fen;
Hath flourish ilk again.
Great joy it is to see, hey ho!

This is a lovely song, worthy of the great tradition
of the Leominster manuscript; but for all its late
date it shows no hint of any development from the
medieval tradition. There is no sense of the inti-
mately human, of the here-and-now: the speaker is
any man, speaking of any nightingale, on any May
morning. To illustrate a new sense of humanity,
contrasting both with the violent Teutonic drama of
" Woefully arrayed " and the lovely lyrical abstrac-

tion of " By a bank as I lay," I quote a famous lyric
of Wyatt.

> *And wilt thou leave me thus?*
> *Say nay, say nay, for shame,*
> *To save thee from the blame*
> *Of all my grief and grame,*
> *And wilt thou leave me thus?*
> *Say nay, say nay!*
>
> *And wilt thou leave me thus,*
> *That hath loved thee so long*
> *In wealth and woe among?*
> *And is thy heart so strong*
> *As for to leave me thus?*
> *Say nay, say nay!*
>
> *And wilt thou leave me thus,*
> *That hath given thee my heart*
> *Never for to depart*
> *Neither for pain nor smart:*
> *And wilt thou leave me thus?*
> *Say nay, say nay!*
>
> *And wilt thou leave me thus*
> *And have no more pity*
> *Of him that loveth thee?*
> *Helas thy cruelty!*
> *And wilt thou leave me thus?*
> *Say nay, say nay!*

Slight as it is, this poem is rich in its implications.
In its economy, its elegance, and its sophistication it

47

contrasts with the clotted strength of "Woefully arrayed." In its dramatic sense, in its creating the dramatic illusion of a real lover pleading with a real woman and of doing so even now, it contrasts with the abstraction of "By a bank as I lay." It does imply some changed sense of human values. I shall spend most of the rest of this chapter in commenting on this change in Wyatt and other Tudor poets.

But before speaking of the different lyric poets I must make a general observation. Up to Wyatt it had been a case not of lyric poets but of lyric poetry; from Wyatt onwards it is the reverse. Of the names of the men who wrote the best medieval lyrics we know nothing, still less of their lives. With the age of Henry VIII we know not only the names but much about the careers of the men who wrote most of the best lyrics. In the section on criticism I shall assert that the characteristic medieval justification of literature was the recreational one and that at the end of the fifteenth century the characteristic justification became more solemn and moral. To an activity taken so lightly as the medieval song, anonymity was appropriate; but to the heavier morality of Renaissance critical theory the responsibility of admitted authorship became more appropriate. Further, it is quite impossible to disengage the lyrics of some of the poets I am about to mention from their characters as seen in action, from their careers. It is partly that we know so much of their lives, from outside sources, and partly that their lives leave their palpable and inescapable impression on their poems. We cannot escape our awareness of Wyatt's powerful personality and the clear and interesting circumstances of his life. We feel his inherited loyalty to the house of Tudor; we know of his unhappy marriage, his visit to Italy and the literary contacts he must have made there, his skill and conscientiousness as a diplomat, his relief when dismissed to retirement to his estate in Kent, where he could live the life of a cultured country gentleman, and his distress of mind when imprisoned on a false charge. All these things force themselves on us if we read his works. And, most vivid of all, Holbein included him among those men and women whose portraits have done so much to make the court life of Henry VIII come alive for us.

The same is true of the Earl of Surrey. We cannot help knowing the kind of man he was and the kind of life he led: a man higher in the social scale and thereby more deeply committed to the perils of political intrigue and ambition than Wyatt; proud to arrogance of his royal descent through his mother and retentive of the forms of medieval chivalry, now growing antiquated; happy in his association with Henry VIII's illegitimate son, the Duke of Richmond, whose chosen companion he was in the chivalrous education appropriate to their station at Windsor Castle and later at the French court; the zealous and skillful commander of an army at Calais; and finally the victim of the groundless suspicions of his royal master through the intrigues of the opposing court party. In the age of Elizabeth it is simply impossible to forget the tragic career of Southwell the Jesuit, while to seek to forget the life of Sidney in reading his works would be a ludicrous waste of energy. For good or ill the lyric has left one area of life and firmly settled itself in another. I am not forgetting the many anonymous Elizabethan lyrics; but, though many, they are not the rule; and those of the first quality are few compared with such poems by known authors.

Having observed this much in general, we can now return to the separate authors and to Wyatt in the first place. I began my remarks on him by quoting a lyric, with deliberate intention: partly to show how original he is, and partly how traditional; for it is in the union of both these qualities that his charm principally lies. As commanding an exquisite sense of the songlike element in the lyric and as writing in a variety of lyric measures, he is the heir of the Leominster songs and the fifteenth-century carols; and as a lyrical dramatist with a sense of the present human situation, he lets the new Renaissance spirit into English poetry. Another reason for beginning with Wyatt's lyrics is that through them one can best counter the persistent heresy that he was no more than a fumbling, if talented, experimenter. So recently as 1947, Mr. G. M. Young, who ought to know better, pronounced to a British Academy audience, who I hope were properly shocked, that " the metrical fumblings of Wyatt and his contemporaries show that the key to the old music had been lost and the key to the new music not yet found." Mr. Young's remarks could apply to a few of Wyatt's sonnets; applied to the lyrics, however, they are the precise contrary to the truth. In the lyric tradition there was no break; the key to the old music was never lost; and Wyatt's lyrics are a very noble example of a lovely metrical tradition maintained, but adapted to a new ethical and social sensibility. Let us look at a second lyric, airy and slight in substance, but illustrating the perfect technical finish and the new dramatic sense. It is a lover's soliloquy, but the dramatic situation is precisely implied. The lover soliloquises after his cheeky mistress has snubbed and left him; and he speaks in an " I ask you " or " What would *you* do about it? " tone.

> *With serving still*
> *This have I won,*
> *For my goodwill*
> *To be undone.*
>
> *And for redress*
> *Of all my pain,*
> *Disdainfulness*
> *I have again;*

And for reward
  Of all my smart,
Lo, thus unheard
  I must depart!

Wherefore all ye
  That after shall
By fortune be,
  As I am, thrall,

Example take
  What I have won
Thus for her sake
  To be undone!

Nothing could be better than the dramatic emphasis of " *This* have I won " and " *Thus* for her sake," or than the skill with which " Disdainfulness " is made to occupy a whole line, suggesting a choking mouthful of very dry biscuit instead of the refreshing drink the lover had hoped for. Moreover, the speaker is half acting. He puts on just a little more indignation than he really feels in order to make his advice to the audience to take example by him the more effective. In fact the humor and the elegant conversational tone are not only new, but look right forward to the witty sophistication of the court lyric of a century later, to a poem like

Why so pale and wan, fond lover,
  Prithee, why so pale?

Will, when looking well can't move her,
Looking ill prevail?
Prithee, why so pale?

Why so dull and mute, young sinner,
Prithee, why so mute?
Will, when speaking well can't win her,
Saying nothing do't?
Prithee, why so mute?

Quit, quit, for shame; this will not move,
This cannot take her;
If of herself she will not love,
Nothing can make her:
The devil take her!

One of the marks of later Renaissance humanism was the turning of the speculative faculty onto the human mind itself; and we are told that Montaigne was the first writer to show it in any eminent degree. Now Wyatt, as well as being dramatic, could be introspective; and I will quote one of his less known lyrics in substantiation. It begins " Spite hath no power to make me sad," and it exhibits a toughness of thought not found in the authentic lyric till the age of Sidney and then not very often. It is more formal and less purely songlike than the poems so far quoted, but there is a strong undercurrent of feeling. Wyatt imagines himself rejected by someone whose love he once possessed and counters rejection by rejection. If, he says, his love had never prospered, he might now be bitter. But he once had what he wished, and, anticipating Browning's doctrine of the eternal moment, that, he says, is as good as having it now. Moreover the lady, through having changed, no longer exists. Her wronging him has wiped out her name.

Spite hath no power to make me sad,
Nor scornfulness to make me plain.
It doth suffice that once I had,
And so to leave, it is no pain.
Let them frown on that least doth gain;
Who did rejoice must needs be glad:
And though with words thou weenest to reign,
It doth suffice that once I had.

Since that in cheeks thus overthwart
And coyly looks thou dost delight,
It doth suffice that mine thou wert,
Though change hath put thy faith to flight.
Alas, it is a peevish spite
To yield thyself and then to part;
But since thou seest thy faith so light,
It doth suffice that mine thou wert.

And since thy love doth thus decline,
And in thy heart such hate doth grow,
It doth suffice that thou wert mine,
And with good will I quite it so.
Sometime my friend, farewell my foe,
Since thou change I am not thine;
But for relief of all my woe
It doth suffice that thou wert mine.

54

Praying you all that hears this song
To judge no wight, nor none to blame:
It doth suffice she doth me wrong,
And that herself doth know the same.
And though she change it is no shame;
Their kind it is and hath been long.
Yet I protest she hath no name;
It doth suffice she doth me wrong.

Many of Wyatt's poems are founded on Italian or French originals; but I have not read that this poem has been traced to any source. It has indeed the mark of independent psychological experience.

It may be a matter of surprise that in seeking the new elements in Wyatt I have gone to poems most in the tradition of the medieval lyric and least in that of the new learning of Italy; for Wyatt's innovation, according to most of the histories, was that he imported the Petrarchian sonnet. Now Wyatt travelled in Italy; he was in touch with the principal source of the new learning; and he did translate some of those sonnets of Petrarch which were so adored and imitated at that time. That he was touched by the luminous and critical spirit of contemporary Italian literature is certain, and yet he showed that spirit more successfully in his medievalizing lyrics than in his would-be Italianate sonnets. The sonnets are uncouth and uninspired works of duty; it was only in the freedom of his native tradition that the lessons he learned in Italy could be applied. Moreover, there was nothing particularly new about the Petrarchian themes. Petrarch's lover who is hot and cold at the same time, who is so near death from love that any further attack his mistress makes on him can only be to torture not to kill, who is like a moth singed in the burning brightness of his lady's eye, is a mere variant of a long established type going back to the Troubadour poets. Petrarch's innovation was stylistic, and that style Wyatt failed to recapture.

I have considered Wyatt before Surrey not only because he was the older man but because he is the greater innovator. Wyatt, so close to the Middle Ages in the lyrical forms he used and prophetic of Donne in the dramatic and introspective substance of his lyrics, extends indeed beyond his age. Surrey, with less originality, is centrally of it. He reminds me of the still prevailing architecture of the age: the late Gothic or Perpendicular varied exceptionally with a little Renaissance ornament. Now characteristic of the Perpendicular style was a liking for balance and repetition. This liking may have been partly economic—it was cheaper to repeat—but it probably grew also from a new desire for balance and harmony, for classical qualities. Surrey's innovation is mainly of such a kind. There is little of the new humanism in him, little of the speculative spirit, but something of the new civilisation that characterized the virtue of courtesy. Surrey's sonnets are far more chastened and ordered than

Wyatt's; and he is at home in translating Martial's quietist, stoical epigram *Ad Seipsum* into the evenly flowing verses of

> *Martial, the things for to attain*
> *The happy life be these, I find.*

The poem that offers the closest analogy with Perpendicular architecture and which I think Surrey's best, is a conventional love lyric in which he compares the delays of his own courtship to the delays experienced by the Greeks in recapturing Helen from the Trojans. The substance is medieval. Troy in the poem is not Homer's but Lydgate's. The war was "all to win a lady fair," and we picture her as in an illuminated manuscript; and it is not leaders or chieftains but knights that wage the war. In contrast, there are many reminiscences of Petrarch suggesting, if you will, the addition of a few Renaissance ornaments. But the virtue of the poem lies in its beautiful balance and disposition. The comparison is faultlessly worked out, and the poem ends logically with a kind of Q. E. D. air. This comparison is between the troubles of the Greeks—the contrary winds, the sacrifice of Iphigenia, the prolongation of the war—before they won back Helen, and the lover's troubles in winning his mistress. The lover is in despair but he is reminded of a greater set of troubles about a lady, the Trojan War about Helen. But these greater troubles were about someone less fair than his mistress. So he has far less reason to complain than the Greeks. Yet the Greeks persisted. So much the more, then, should he. And he ends with the resolve to go on hoping. The poem consists of only two sentences: one immensely long comprising four stanzas, and the other comprising the fifth and last.

When raging love with extreme pain
Most cruelly distrains my heart,
When that my tears, as floods of rain,
Bear witness of my woful smart,
When sighs have wasted so my breath
That I lie at the point of death;

I call to mind the navy great
That the Greeks brought to Troye town
And how the boisterous winds did beat
Their ships and rent their sails adown,
Till Agamemnon's daughter's blood
Appeased the gods that them withstood;

And how that in those ten years' war
Full many a bloody deed was done,
And many a lord, that came full far,
There caught his bane, alas, too soon,
And many a good knight overrun,
Before the Greeks had Helen won;

Then think I thus: sith such repair,
So long time war of valiant men,
Was all to win a lady fair,

Shall I not learn to suffer then
And think my life well spent to be
Serving a worthier wight than she?

Therefore I never will repent,
But pains, contented, still endure;
For like as when, rough winter spent,
The pleasant spring straight draweth in ure,
So after raging storms of care
Joyful at length may be my fare.

There is no drama, no sense of the here-and-now in this poem, but it is a highly reasonable, civilized affair, the kind of thing that would have earned the approval of an Augustan poet.

That, then, is what Surrey is mainly good for, but it would be unfair to him not to mention first an exception to his lack of drama, and second a very remarkable innovation of his in a single department.

One of Surrey's best poems, rightly honored by most anthologists, is that beginning "O happy dames." It is a soliloquy of a wife whose husband is absent, comparing her lot with that of happier women whose husbands are at home. It contains a highly dramatic picture of the anxious wife standing at the window watching the weather.

When other lovers, in arms across,
Rejoice their chief delight,
Drowned in tears, to mourn my loss
I stand the bitter night

In my window, where I may see
Before the winds how the clouds flee.
Lo, what a mariner love hath made me!

And in green waves when the salt flood
Doth rise by rage of wind,
A thousand fancies in that mood
Assail my restless mind.
Alas! now drencheth my sweet foe,
That with the spoil of my heart did go,
And left me; but, alas, why did he so?

And when the seas wax calm again
To chase from me annoy,
My doubtful hope doth cause me plain;
So dread cuts off my joy.
Thus is my wealth mingled with woe,
And of each thought a doubt doth grow:
Now he comes; will he come? alas, no, no!

Surrey's innovation has to do with nature. It is a general truth that until the eighteenth century, English poets were unable to objectify nature, to see it in detachment. Usually they treated nature in an emblematic way, making it illustrate a moral or at least subserve something else appropriately. Henryson at the beginning of his *Testament of Cresseid* says that a doleful season should be made to fit a doleful ditty; and he proceeds to describe the frosty evening on which he read the unhappy story of Cresseid's punishment. And, we learn later, the

weather was frosty not only because frost is generally unpleasant and hence appropriate to the unhappy
tale, but because Saturn was a frosty planet and it
was Saturn who smote Cresseid with leprosy. So,
convincingly though Henryson describes the cold
evening, his description is anything but detached.
This medieval habit extended right beyond Surrey.
Here, for instance, is a natural description in Sack-
ville's " Induction to his Tragedy of Buckingham "
in the *Mirror for Magistrates*, where its moral
application is plainly specified:

> *And sorrowing I to see the summer flowers,*
> *The lively green, the lusty leas forlorn,*
> *The sturdy trees so shatter'd with the showers,*
> *The fields so fade that flourish'd so beforn,*
> *It taught me well, all earthly things be born*
> *To die the death, for nought may long time last;*
> *The summer's beauty yields to winter's blast.*
>
> *And looking upward to the heaven's leams*
> *With nightes stars thick powder'd everywhere,*
> *Which erst so glisten'd with the golden streams*
> *That cheerful Phoebus spread down from his sphere,*
> *Beholding dark oppressing day so near,*
> *The sudden sight reduced to my mind*
> *The sundry changes that on earth we find.*

But in a few passages in Surrey we find nature
described in a totally new way. Here is the best
example of all: the beginning of one of the sonnets
he translated from Petrarch:

Alas! so all things now do hold their peace:
Heaven and earth disturbed in no thing,
The beasts, the air; the birds their song do cease,
The nightes car the stars about doth bring;
Calm is the sea, the waves work less and less.

It is true that this description is subordinated to the whole sonnet, which exploits the contrast between the calm of nature and the unrest of the lover's mind. And in Petrarch's poem this subordination is complete. But Surrey alters Petrarch with startling effect. First, he expands Petrarch's nature description by one line, and second he alters Petrarch's simple statement that the sea lies in its bed, waveless, to " calm is the sea, the waves work less and less." Now the last phrase is a wonderful rendering of a piece of sheer, detached, natural observation. Nothing could give better the impression of a sea sinking into calm than the phrase, " the waves work less and less." Such a sea does present itself to us as tired and worked out and sinking into quietude through exhaustion. And the touch is gratuitous; it does not correspond to any statement that, on the contrary, the passions in the lover's heart are beginning to increase in violence.

If you want to see the qualities of Wyatt and Surrey and the shares they have in promoting the Renaissance in England, consider this contemporary analogy. Wyatt, though his lyrics may be small, even fragile affairs, resembles Thomas More; Surrey resembles Elyot, author of the *Governor*. More is at once rooted in the Middle Ages and highly prophetic of an enlargement of human sympathies that was only to take place much later. He also shows a very keen sense of drama, of the here-and-now, in his introduction to *Utopia* and in his *History of Richard III*. Elyot is a man of his age, civilized but rather static, anecdotal and homiletic rather than dramatic, influenced by the matter of the new learning but at heart far more of a conservative than More.

In the age that followed, the age of the great translators and of the *Mirror for Magistrates*, the lyric tradition of Wyatt declined, to be resumed with increased energy in the great Elizabethan age. In that age the bulk of the lyric is not noticeably humanistic or dramatic: it unites the great songlike tradition with the subject matter of Petrarch and of the pastoral. Such a masterpiece of lyric beauty as the following just does not come within the scope of the Renaissance movements I have been outlining, or only in ways too subtle for exposition:

> *O Love! they wrong thee much*
> *That say thy sweet is bitter,*
> *When thy rich fruit is such*
> *As nothing can be sweeter.*
> *Fair house of joy and bliss,*
> *Where truest pleasure is,*
> *I do adore thee:*

I know thee what thou art,
I serve thee with my heart,
And fall before thee.

No, it is not the songbooks generally that carry on the intellectualizing and dramatic sides of Wyatt, but one or two of the court-poets: Raleigh, Dyer, Greville, and above all Sidney.

There are also the recusant poets, the circumstances of whose lives forced them away from the airier modes of Petrarch and the pastoral and towards the more sober and realistic portion of Wyatt's verse. It is also quite natural that these poets, when not resorting to continental sources, should prolong an earlier, not adopt the fashionable contemporary, lyric tradition. The fine poem by Southwell, the aristocratic Englishman who was also a Jesuit priest and an emissary from his order to his own country, on the thoughts aroused by contemplating a skull is very much in the Wyatt tradition with its realism and artfully varied refrain.

Before my face the picture hangs
That daily should put me in mind
Of those cold names and bitter pangs
That shortly I am like to find:
But yet, alas, full little I
Do think hereon that I must die.

Continually at my bed's head
An hearse doth hang, which doth me tell

That I ere morning may be dead,
Though now I feel myself full well:
But yet, alas, for all this I
Have little mind that I must die.

The gown which I do use to wear,
The knife wherewith I cut my meat,
And eke that old and ancient chair
Which is my only usual seat,
All these do tell me I must die,
And yet my life amend not I.

The sense of present life, of the here-and-now of these lines, worthily continues the pattern set by Wyatt.

Let us turn finally to Sidney, greatest of the court poets.

Like Wyatt, Sidney was a great experimenter and was familiar with Italian. He could be academic and fantastic and formal at times, just as in his *Arcadia* he could be outrageously ingenious and improbable. On the other hand, as *Arcadia* has a very real contemporary political application, and as its conventional sentiments can give way to poignant drama—for example when Pamela and Philoclea suffer imprisonment and persecution—so in the lyric Sidney can assure us of his closeness to actual life, of his dramatic sense. I will end this chapter by describing and quoting a lyric of Sidney's which is both songlike and dramatic, and which, through its union of medievalism and novelty, illustrates my recurrent theme in these chapters: namely, the eleventh song in *Astrophel and Stella* beginning, " Who is it that this dark night? " It is a serenade in the form of the lover (or Astrophel) pleading outside the mistress's (or Stella's) window at night; but it is also a formal dialogue between the two, the lady speaking the first two lines and the lover the last three of each stanza. This form of argument or debate is thoroughly medieval; yet the five line stanza is, I believe, original and a wonderfully effective invention. The rhyme-scheme is *ababa* and the last line, echoing lines one and three and not closed by a third *b* rhyme, is like a melancholy echo. The *b* rhymes are all double (as the *a* rhymes are all single) and fuller in sound; the absence of the third *b* rhyme is hence all the more felt. There is great dramatic power. The trochaic rhythm expresses hurry and excitement; and the manipulation of the words suggests a whispered conversation.

> " *Who is it that this dark night*
> *Underneath my window plaineth?* "
> *It is one who from thy sight*
> *Being, ah, exil'd, disdaineth*
> *Every other vulgar light.*

> " *Why, alas, and are you he?*
> *Be not yet those fancies changed?* "
> *Dear, when you find change in me,*
> *Though from me you be estranged,*
> *Let my change to ruin be.*

66

"Well, in absence this will die;
Leave to see and leave to wonder."
Absence sure will help, if I
Can learn how myself to sunder
From what in my heart doth lie.

"But time will these thoughts remove;
Time doth work what no man knoweth."
Time doth as the subject prove;
With time still the affection groweth
In the faithful turtle-dove.

"What if we new beauties see,
Will not they stir new affection?"
I will think they pictures be
(Image-like, of saints' perfection)
Poorly counterfeiting thee.

"But your reason's purest light
Bids you leave such minds to nourish."
Dear, do reason no such spite;
Never doth thy beauty flourish
More than in my reason's sight.

"But the wrongs Love bears will make
Love at length leave undertaking."
No, the more fools it doth shake,
In a ground of so firm making
Deeper still they drive the stake.

"Peace, I think that some give ear.
Come no more, lest I get anger."
Bliss, I will my bliss forbear;
Fearing, sweet, you to endanger;
But my soul shall harbour there.

" Well, be gone; be gone I say,
Lest that Argus' eyes perceive you."
Oh unjust is Fortune's sway,
Which can make me thus to leave you,
And from louts to run away.

III

Criticism

I USE the word criticism in a restricted sense. For instance, I am not dealing with applied criticism, that is the criticism of texts, of which indeed there was little, and of that very little good, in the periods under review; nor am I dealing with theories of language—whether you should use Latin or your own vernacular—nor with theories of rhetoric. Instead I am thinking of how the ordinary thoughtful man would justify literature, of what answer he would give to the Philistine or the Puritan who asked him what good was it. I say " thoughtful man " because even in so religious a century as the thirteenth or in so severely moral a century as the sixteenth there were plenty of the profane who wanted to write recreational or amatory or scurrilous or satirical verse or to listen to it, and were not to be put off by all the clerics in Christendom. And for these it mattered little whether their more staid contemporaries justified poetry or not, or on what grounds they did so. Like Catullus with his Lesbia, they were in love with their profane Muse, and valued all the murmurings of the strait-laced old men at exactly one penny. But such folk, the rebels, the literary Falstaffs of the world, are a constant; and though, to keep our sense of proportion, we should not forget their unbroken existence, their very constancy robs them of historical interest. So let us return to the ordinary thoughtful man and see whether his thoughts about how you can justify literature changed through the ages under review.

Beginning with the noon of the Middle Ages we find, along with a wonderful output of creative work, the most astonishing confusions and contradictions of theory. It was a contradiction of long standing. St. Jerome had both quoted Virgil and denounced the pagan writers. Ovid's *Art of Love* and Martial's *Epigrams* were found with the Bible and the Fathers in monastic libraries. As Comparetti said, " While the ancients are steadily hated and maligned as pagans, their works are assiduously read and studied, and they are looked up to by the most enlightened Christians as men of learning and genius." There is the same contradiction in Chaucer. He gave the best part of himself to poetry and at the end of the *Canterbury Tales* in his " retraction" he called his poems his " guilts" and asked God to pardon him for them. But in spite of this confusion, and if you are content to follow, not the handbooks on rhetoric but the hints dropped in various places, you can gather a few rough truths about how literature was regarded in the Middle Ages.

First, there was the pervasive influence of the medieval church. As soon as men began reflecting at all about the justification of literature, they automatically took the church into account. The church on its own side looked on literature somewhat as it looked on the sexual instincts: wholly bad if indulged in without regulation, good if indulged in under proper rules, though less good than abstention. C. S. Lewis in his *Allegory of Love* has written interestingly of the medieval church's jealousy of marriage. It feared excessive marital affection as likely to interfere with the devotion man owed to his church and his maker: a fear faithfully inherited by Milton in *Paradise Lost* when he makes God blame Adam's yielding to Eve in the words,

> *Was shee thy God, that her thou didst obey*
> *Before his voice?*

Just so the church was jealous of any very high claims made for the virtue of literature and was correspondingly more favorable to justifying poetry for marginal or superficial reasons. The old notion of the poet as the prophet or inspired teacher was not dead in the Middle Ages, but it was frowned on and incurred violent opposition. On the other hand the church did not object to literature being a humble and subordinate ally; and it is truly symbolical of this state of affairs that a good deal of medieval literature was the work of men in minor orders. *Cursor Mundi* is a long narrative poem dealing with scriptural history, the material of the Miracle Play cycles. At the beginning the author says he is writing for ignorant Englishmen in the hope of amending their lives and keeping them from vanities. The church would have approved of the poem as a legitimate if inferior means of doing what the preachers did in their sermons: something parallel to the representation of the same episodes on the stage, or in paint on the church walls, or in glass in the church windows.

Another legitimate use of literature was to commemorate the acts of great men and women, whether saints or figures in secular history. Here was a useful recording work which did not come into competition with ecclesiastical preserves. But the most characteristic of all medieval justifications of literature was what they would have called "honest mirth." Aquinas himself had set his confirmation on the truth that you cannot keep the soul always at a stretch and that play is necessary for human nature. Here is a justification the remotest possible from the ideas of the poet-prophet and of poetry as a high exercise of the soul, and one which need cause the church not the least uneasiness. It was perfectly apt that Chaucer, if he chose to put his most didactic

72

tale into the mouth of one cleric, the Parson, put one of his most amusing (if innocently amusing) tales into the mouth of another cleric, the Nuns' Priest. This tale could indeed stand as a classic instance of that honest mirth approved of by medieval orthodoxy; it gives perfectly the Aquinian relaxation.

A famous passage in Langland's *Piers Plowman* is most instructive. It is at the beginning of the splendid passus where the allegorical figure called Imaginative (meaning memory and reflection) reproves the poet for spending time over his verses:

> *And thou meddlest thee with makings, and*
> *mightest go say thy psalter*
> *And bid for them that giveth thee bread;*
> *for there are books enough*
> *To tell men what Do-well is.*

To which the poet retorts with the proverb of Cato: *interpone tuis interdum gaudia curis* ("from time to time punctuate your serious affairs with pleasure"). Thus Langland's defense of his poem is that it is a piece of legitimate relaxation amid more serious affairs. And he was the man about whom a modern Catholic historian, Christopher Dawson, wrote:

Here is the Catholic Englishman *par excellence*, at once the most English of Catholic poets and the most Catholic of English poets: a man in whom Catholic faith and national feeling are fused in a single flame. He saw Christ walking in English fields in the dress of an English labourer, and to understand his work is to know English religion in its most autochthonous and yet most Catholic form.

So what a contrast with this is Langland's own self-justification of his poem to contemporary Catholic orthodoxy. Not a word about his poem being an attempt at a great religious work; not a hint that it can even begin to do the work represented by his saying his psalter: only the humble plea that his trivial verses may be excused as legitimate relaxation for the writer.

This posture of humility before the church was, I believe, truly characteristic of medieval literature, and it makes medieval critical ideas genuinely different from those of the Renaissance. Langland and Sidney belonged to different critical worlds.

How did the change begin? Less perhaps through the more widely accepted notion of classical influence than through the transference of some authority from ecclesiastical to secular things. One of the legitimate concerns of literature had been the record and celebration of the doings of great men. Such a concern was continued through poetry and history during the centuries that followed Chaucer and Langland, but with a different emphasis. In the Middle Ages the emphasis was on fact, and on record, and on pleasure. As the years went on, as nationalism encroached on the idea of an undivided Western Christendom, as kings became less amenable to papal discipline, the emphasis changed. Some of the seriousness that had forsaken clerical affairs was transferred to secular; the accounts of great men became more solemn, less recreational, and more didactic. You can see the change in Petrarch and Boccaccio in Italy, and with the natural time lag, in Lydgate's adaptations of Boccaccio in English. History and poems about great men became less a factual or diverting chronicle and more a series of object lessons, either of what to imitate or of what to avoid. In the fifteenth century men felt themselves terribly dependent on the character that their ruler happened to possess, and they believed that the ruler's character might really be influenced by the examples of virtue and vice he met in literature. One of the best places to observe this change of temper is in the prefaces Caxton attached to the popular works he printed for the first time in his printing press. One of these works was the history of Godfrey of Boulogne, one of the leaders of the First Crusade. The age for which this romance was written considered it chiefly as a matter of recreation; but Caxton states that this book was

reduced out of French into English to the end that every Christian man may be the better encouraged to enterprise war for the defence of Christendom and to recover the city of Jerusalem.

Another book Caxton printed was *Reynard the Fox,*

and again he omits any recreational notion and says
solemnly that the object of the volume is to put men
on their guard against the many deceits that are
practised in the world. A third book is Higden's
universal history, *Polycronicon*, and in his long and
earnest preface Caxton makes it clear that this is no
mere record but a work of great didactic importance
showing the reader " what thing is to be desired and
what is to be eschewed."

This stern didactic spirit, now reinforced by
Protestant zeal, comes out in the next century in
Roger Ascham and his denunciation of medieval
romances. What had once satisfied religious vigi-
lance on grounds of pleasure and recreation fails to
satisfy the sterner morality and more didactic temper
of a rather less religious age. I quote, not Ascham's
more famous attack on *Morte d'Arthur* in the *School-
master*, but his less known words to the same effect
in his preface to *Toxophilus*, addressed " to all the
gentlemen and yeomen of England ":

In our fathers' time nothing was read but books of feigned
chivalry, wherein a man by reading should be led to no
other end but only to manslaughter and bawdry. If any
man suppose they were good enough to pass the time
withal he is deceived, for surely vain words do work no
small thing in vain ignorant and young minds, specially
if they be given anything thereunto of their own nature.
These books, as I have heard say, were made the most

76

part in abbeys and monasteries, a very likely and fit fruit of such an idle and blind kind of living.

It is to about the same period that those two typical pieces of Renaissance didacticism in England belong: the *Mirror for Magistrates* and *Gorboduc*. The first is a vast series of tales about princes and statesmen who came to a bad end, and the account of their deaths had the same object as that attributed to the court of justice that caused Admiral Byng to be executed: to inspire the rest with courage. The second, narrating the internecine war of Ferrex and Porrex, whom King Gorboduc unwisely made joint heirs of his kingdom, was aimed directly at Queen Elizabeth, being a dreadful object lesson of what happens to a country when the succession is not sure, and an incitement to her to avoid such disasters by marrying and thus securing the succession.

These two pieces of literature show not only a critical emphasis different from the medieval but a different critical state of affairs. In the Middle Ages, the rules of rhetoric apart, literature was made first; and criticism, if any, had to make the best of what literature was already there. By the middle of the sixteenth century, critical theory began to influence literary production. At any rate, the *Mirror for Magistrates* and *Gorboduc* are exceptionally conscious of the kind of thing the literary theory of the time required. Somewhat paradoxically the medi-

eval method was more *human*, in the sense of answering to the casual and opportunist side of human
nature which is one of the things that stops man
being a machine; while the early Elizabethan method
showed an advance in *humanism* because it illustrated a wider assertion of human rights, albeit
rather rigidly applied.

I come now to English Renaissance criticism
proper, and to the two great figures, Puttenham and
Sidney. Campion and Daniel conducted a charming,
well-bred, and illuminating controversy, but it is a
limited affair compared with the *Art of English
Poesy* and the *Defence of Poetry*.

One of the most interesting recent discoveries
about English literature is that published in 1936
about Puttenham's *Art of English Poesy*. In the
preface to their edition of this work, Miss Willcock
and Miss Walker prove that the bulk of it belongs to
the fifteen sixties and not to the fifteen eighties as
previously thought and that it is the critical counterpart not of *Euphues* and the *Fairy Queen* but of
Tottell's " Miscellany," the *Mirror for Magistrates*,
and the early translations. Seen thus it evades comparison with Sidney's better known work and is
found to be a fine example of pre-Euphuistic prose
and nearer akin, as prose, to Cavendish's *Life of
Wolsey* than to Sidney's *Arcadia*. It is a far more
original piece of writing than Lodge's *Defence of*

78

Poetry and Webbe's *Discourse of English Poetry*, with which it was apt to be associated.

For anyone who has carried to excess the idea that the Renaissance is no more than the natural sequence of the Middle Ages, I recommend first the effort to gather the sense of what the Middle Ages thought about literature and then a reading or re-reading of the first book of Puttenham and of Sidney's *Defence*. One of the common ways to prove such a sequence is to point out how much of classical literature was known to the Middle Ages and to be scornful of those picturesque accounts, once so popular, of the ferment of excitement in the Western world, and Italy in particular, when a forgotten Greek or Roman author was brought to light; thereby insinuating that what of classical literature was added to the existing medieval store was not of paramount importance. But when you try to apply the procedure to literary criticism, it simply will not work. In Renaissance criticism the difference of feeling is startling, and the classical influence, scanty in the Middle Ages, is now conspicuous. I shall quote Puttenham in support of this statement, but I must give warning that he is exceptional among Elizabethan critics. First, in belonging to the age just before the outbursts of Puritan hostility to the stage, he can take for granted a more solid predisposition towards literature and be less on the defensive. Secondly, he is closer to Aristotle than any Elizabethan critic; and conspicuously in these two ways.

First, he insists on showing and, in doing so, on approving the sheer fact that poetry is a considerable ingredient in human life; and secondly, he is prone to think of poetry largely in terms of the human mind and not as something conveying from this or that authority certain lessons that have to be imposed on mankind for their good. In his exordium Puttenham repeats what was indeed by now a commonplace in Europe that

the profession and use of poesy is most ancient from the beginning and not, as many erroneously suppose, after but before any civil society was among men. For it is written that poesy was the original cause and occasion of their first assemblies when before the people remained in the woods and mountains, vagrant and dispersed like the wild beasts, lawless and naked or very ill clad, and of all good and necessary provision for harbour or sustenance utterly unfurnished, so as they little differed from the very brutes of the field. Whereupon it is feigned that Amphion and Orpheus, two poets of the first ages, one of them, to wit Amphion, builded up cities and reared walls with the stones that came in heaps to the sound of his harp, figuring thereby the mollifying of hard and stony hearts by his sweet and eloquent persuasion. And Orpheus assembled the wild beasts to come in herds to hearken to his music and by this means made them tame, implying thereby how by his discreet and wholesome lessons uttered in harmony and with melodious instruments he brought the rude and savage people to a more civil and orderly life.

And Puttenham goes on to say that poets were the first astronomers, inventors of religious ceremonies, and ministers of the holy mysteries. They were even the first devisers of laws. Now all this is much more than Aristotle said, and Puttenham did not invent the sentiments. But by the luminous and assured way he speaks Puttenham produces the equivalent of Aristotle's serene assurance, his absolute taking for granted, that poetry is one of other matters—ethics, rhetoric, and politics for instance —with which all men are concerned, and have to be concerned if they are to be whole human beings and are not to stunt their natures. Puttenham makes this claim more explicitly in his remarkable section on the imagination. The imagination, he says, is a faculty which can run riot and distort reality, but it is also a faculty without which the mind is unable to create at all. When the imagination is " well affected " it is

not only nothing disorderly or confused with any monstrous imaginations or conceits but very formal (*i. e.* orderly) and in his much multiformity uniform and so passing clear that by it, as by a glass or mirror, are represented unto the soul all manner of beautiful visions, whereby the inventive part of the mind is so much holpen as without it no man could devise any new or rare thing; and where it is not excellent in his kind there could be no politic captain nor any witty enginer or cunning artificer, nor yet any lawmaker or counsellor of deep disclosure.

81

By making the imagination an essential means to *all* creative work, poetic and practical alike, Puttenham clearly reinforces the Aristotelian assumptions. But this same passage illustrates also Puttenham's other Aristotelian quality of putting poetry in terms of the mind. Later he justifies certain types of poetry not for any specific lesson they convey but for the general benefit they bring to the mind's health. The poetry of public rejoicing, whether for triumphs, installations, birthdays or weddings, gets its justification from serving a great principle of the human mind.

Pleasure is the chief part of man's felicity in this world and also (as our theologians say) in the world to come. Therefore, while we may (yea always if it could be), to rejoice and take our pleasures in virtuous and honest sort it is not only allowable but also necessary and very natural to man. And many be the joys and consolations of the heart, but none greater than such as he may utter and discover by some convenient means; even as to suppress and hide a man's mirth and not to have therein a partaker, or at least a witness, is no little grief and infelicity.

And after enlarging on rejoicings and their poetical celebration, he goes on to their opposite and says:

Lamenting is altogether contrary to rejoicing; every man says so, and yet it is a piece of joy to be able to lament with ease and freely to pour forth a man's inward sorrows and the griefs wherewith his mind is surcharged.

82

Thus to rejoice and to lament through poetical celebration has nothing to do with a moral but has a cathartic effect similar to that which Aristotle attributes to tragedy.

Here we are far removed from the permissive, often grudgingly permissive, recreational theories of the Middle Ages. Then, poetry of a subordinate kind could be admitted to help the soul in the short periods when theological authority allows it to relax: now, poetry is a great means of health to the soul in its normal activities. Classical antiquity has indeed reasserted itself.

This joyful assertion by Puttenham of the rights of poetry reappears in an unlikely place, close in date to the *Art of English Poesy*. In general the *Mirror for Magistrates* reflects not any new classicizing tendency but the tendency, found first in Lydgate, to transfer some of the awe that pervaded theology to the severe moral lessons that the ruling class could derive from the unfortunate ends of those of its predecessors who acted ill. But among the stories added to the edition of 1563—and hence dating between then and the original edition of 1559—is one of the poet Collingbourne, who got into trouble through the couplet he wrote about the political set-up of England under Richard III:

> *The Cat, the Rat, and Lovel our Dog*
> *Do rule all England under a Hog,*

83

the Hog being Richard, whose emblem was a boar's head. In telling his own sad story Collingbourne not only remarks how careful poets should be to be tactful in their attempts to amend abuses, to "sauce" their poems "so that few need be offended," but inserts under the allegory of the winged Pegasus an eloquent declaration of the poet's full and true scope. It is close in spirit and even expression to Puttenham's first chapter and at once so beautiful and so interesting that I am surprised it does not figure in any of the best known anthologies of English verse or Gregory Smith's *Elizabethan Critical Essays*. I will remind you of the mythological references before I quote the passage. Pegasus, the winged horse, was the offspring of the Ocean-god, Poseidon, and of Medusa; and we must remember that Medusa was a beautiful young woman till she bore Pegasus. It was only after this event that she acquired snaky locks and a petrifying face. The chastity attributed to her by the poet could only be comparative, because she failed in the end to resist the advances of Poseidon. Pegasus used his wings to mount to the heavenly abodes of the gods, which he made his home. But on earth he was associated with the Muses. He was present at the contest between them and the nine daughters of Pierus on Mount Helicon, and it was then that the spring of poetic inspiration, Hippocrene, arose from the dint of his hoof.

84

THE CRITICISM

The Greeks do paint a poet's office whole
In Pegasus, their feigned horse with wings,
Whom, shaped so, Medusa's blood did foal,
Who with his feet strake out the Muses' springs
Fro flinty rocks to Helicon that clings;
And then flew up unto the starry sky,
And there abides among the heavens high.

For he that shall a perfect poet be
Must first be bred out of Medusa's blood;
He must be chaste and virtuous as was she,
Who to her power the Ocean-god withstood;
To th'end also his doom be just and good,
He must, as she had, have one only eye,
Regard of truth, that nought may lead awry.

In courage eke he must be like a horse;
He may not fear to register the right:
And, that no power or fancy do him force,
No bit nor rein his tender jaws may twite.
He must be arm'd with strength of wit and sprite
To dash the rocks, dark causes and obscure,
Till he attain the springs of truth most pure.

His hooves must also pliant be and strong
To rive the rocks of lust and errors blind
In brainless heads, that always wander wrong;
These must he brise with reasons plain and kind,
Till springs of grace do gush out of the mind.
For, till affections from the fond be driven,
In vain is truth told or good counsel given.

85

Like Pegasus a poet must have wings
To fly to heaven, thereto to feed and rest:
He must have knowledge of eternal things;
Almighty love must harbour in his breast.
With worldly cares he may not be oppress'd;
The wings of skill and hope must heave him higher
Than all the joys which worldly wits desire.

He must be also nimble, free, and swift
To travel far to view the trades of men;
Great knowledge oft is gotten by the shift:
Things notable he must be quick to pen,
Reproving vices sharply now and then.
He must be swift when touched tyrants chafe,
To gallop thence, to keep his carcass safe.

The author of this section of the *Mirror for Magistrates* is unknown. But he must have known Plato's *Ion* (with its reference to the poet as etherial and winged) and the doctrine of Plotinus concerning the true poet's intuitive knowledge of eternal things.

We come finally again to Sidney as we have in both of the other two chapters; and here we have a criticism richer and more complicated. In Puttenham it was easier to find simple and striking contrasts with the medieval temper; he is a more purely Renaissance figure. Sidney, great man as he is, gives to his criticism the same range that Milton gave to his epic. Milton was in the advance guard of his age through casting his epic in the strict neoclassic form; he was daringly individual in flouting

the traditional association of the epic with rhyme;
but he was mediéval in going behind the Renaissance
vogue of the heroic story to that of world history
and the pilgrimage of the human soul. Just so
Sidney is entirely up-to-date, indeed in the very advance guard of critical opinion, but at the same time
he casts over his *Defence*, for all its brilliance and
charm, an air of piety that makes us feel that he is
after all the heir of the Middle Ages. The man who
wrote the *Defence* is the man who translated Philippe
de Mornay's work concerning the " Trueness " of
the Christian religion and who took as his starting
point those arguments against poetry which Gosson,
however much of a Protestant, derived ultimately
from Catholic and not from reformed Puritanism.
And it is this piety that, coexisting with all the other
diverse virtues of the *Defence*—the assimilation of
Aristotle, the tempering of Plato by Plotinus, the
breadth of mind that can enjoy at once the simplicity
of the ballad and the mature didacticism of Plutarch
—unites poetry not only with virtuous action but
with the doctrinal requirements of an age that had
inherited some measure of medieval otherworldliness.

That Sidney really meant us to link critical
theory with religious dogma is evident not through
any heavy stress or obtrusive iteration. Sidney
writes as a courtier, and the courtier's *sprezzatura*,
or nonchalance, would forbid anything in the least
reminiscent of a theological treatise. But in two pas-

sages, at least, there are the profoundest implications. One of these concerns the goal of all learning, poetry being a very eminent branch of learning.

This purifying of wit, this enriching of memory, enabling of judgment, and enlarging of conceit, which commonly we call learning, under what name soever it come forth, or to what immediate end soever it be directed, the final end is to lead and draw us to as high a perfection as our degenerate souls, made worse by their clayey lodgings, can be capable of.

I have no doubt that by " degenerate " Sidney meant not just " fallen into evil habits " but incriminated by the sin of Adam, and that " perfection " refers simultaneously to the prelapsarian state in Paradise and to the Platonic good. But it is the second passage that causes me to have no doubts. Sidney is here pleading that the poet goes beyond nature and in so doing has something godlike about him.

Neither let it be deemed too saucy a comparison to balance the highest point of man's wit with the efficacy of Nature, but rather give right honour to the heavenly Maker of that maker, who, having made man to His own likeness, set him beyond and over all the works of that second nature: which in nothing he sheweth so much as in poetry, when with the force of a divine breath he bringeth things forth far surpassing her doings; with no small argument to the incredulous of that first accursed fall of Adam, sith our erected wit maketh us know what perfection is and yet our infected will keepeth us from reaching unto it. But these arguments will by few be understood and by fewer granted.

If Sidney thought few of his readers would understand his argument, it behoves an interpreter to say how he at least takes it. Sidney asserts that it is not impudent to compare the highest reach of man's mind with the creative power of Nature (*natura naturans*). On the contrary it is fitting to praise God for setting him over the natural creation (*natura naturata*). And this superiority comes out in poetry above all, for in poetry man creates things better than can be found in nature—more lovely scenery and people nearer perfection. This creative power confirms the theological doctrine of a perfect state from which man fell, for there must be a connection between the only two perfect states that have been apprehended by man: his perfection in Adam and Eve before they fell and the perfection to which his understanding can reach in the imaginings of poetry. Poetry can glimpse this prelapsarian perfection (which is also the good of the Platonists) even if man's will is too tainted to force him to live up to his vision. The argument is completed by the first passage quoted above. Through learning, of which poetry is a most eminent part, man's will does actually propel his soul some way towards the perfection his understanding has succeeded in glimpsing.

We have seen that from such critical hints as

exist in the Middle Ages we could infer that poetry could be justified on grounds of inspiration, morality, record, and recreation. In including all these grounds in his *Defence*, Sidney is the heir of the Middle Ages; in grading and blending them in an original and undreamed of manner he does indeed indicate that there was such a thing as an English Renaissance.

IV

The Epic

IN DEALING with the epic I at once incur a difficulty that was absent from the other chapters. No one doubts that the Middle Ages produced much lyric writing and at least some scraps of criticism. But it might reasonably be held that they produced no epic whatever, their greatest narrative writing being allegory and not epic at all, and even their best heroic romances not being of that seriousness to touch the true epic elevation. And remember that I am treating of the developed Middle Ages, of the epoch to which the origins of humanism go back, and not of the prolongation of the old Germanic world. The *Song of Roland* and the Norse sagas do not fall within my scope. Now if the critic who denies to the developed Middle Ages any epic creation does so on the premise that the epic and the heroic poem are synonymous, then I have no quarrel with his conclusions. On the other hand I do find his premise, though perfectly workable, narrow and

unphilosophical. And I believe we shall think more
wisely on literary matters, if we define the epic not
by a type of subject-matter, the heroic event, but by
an inner spirit that may find other embodiments than
the heroic poem. I shall have to spend a large part
of this chapter in justifying my position. Only then
can I speak of the transition from the English epic
in the Middle Ages to the English epic in the Renaissance.

It is easy to see why epic and heroic poem were
equated. It so happens that the *Iliad* and the *Odys-
sey* are both, and that Virgil, who was quite capable
of writing a very great narrative on a subject not
strictly heroic, chose to imitate Homer in this respect.
Very naturally people assumed that what might in
fact turn out to be only an adjunct, the heroic subject, was an organic part of the epic effect. Further,
in the nineteenth century men thought more of
Homer and less of Virgil and added the notion that
a poem had a better chance of being epic as it was
more primitive: an idea fostered by the mistaken
assumption that Homer himself (or rather what the
nineteenth century pictured as the " Homeric Com-
mittee ") was very close to the heroic age he described. The result was that people took it for
granted that a heroic episode like the Old English
Battle of Maldon was epic in a way in which the
Fairy Queen could not begin to be. Even so large-
minded a writer as W. P. Ker in so fine a book as

Epic and Romance betrays the influence of such a prejudice. He first talks of an epic age, by which he means one of social primitiveness, and then goes on to postulate for the epic poem things which have nothing to do with the primitive: namely the sense of dignity and the energy belonging to a great age of history, and the power of dealing simply and directly with the great human passions and of creating great characters. Surely this is to pursue incompatible methods of procedure, when the only rational method is to chose between them. Either, if you will, equate epic with heroic and relegate the epic to those pieces of narrative literature that succeed in dealing with a heroic age; or separate the heroic age from the epic altogether and base epic on requirements that have no exclusive connection with any such age. Since I choose the second alternative, it is plainly my business now to say what I think these requirements to be.

Literary definitions, if they are to be anything but academic and hypothetical, must be drawn from actual works of literature. I draw my notion of the epic from a wider field than the heroic poem. I derive it also from certain great verse narratives other than the heroic, and from certain prose narratives both fictional and historical. Thus certain novels are in their essence closer to certain verse narratives than they are to some of their fellow novels. The novel indeed appropriated during the eighteenth and nineteenth centuries large literary areas that had been the property of comic and tragic drama and of the narrative in verse. The case of " epic " is very much that of " classical " and " romantic." As first used by the Germans near the beginning of the nineteenth century, " classical " meant Greek and Latin, " romantic " the Gothic stuff that came after. Now, in Middleton Murry's words, " classical " and " romantic " are " perennial modes of the human spirit." " Epic," too, is a " perennial mode," finding embodiment in a variety of forms. It is a complicated mode, which cannot be simply defined in a few words. I go on to a list of what I think the epic requirements.

The first epic requirement is the simple one of sheer quality. It is just conceivable, though superlatively improbable, that the other conditions required to give the epic effect could be fulfilled by mediocre means. Hence the need to insist that the parts of a work, the language, the structure, and so on, should be excellent in themselves, if the epic effect is to be reached. To insist on quality excludes from the epic category, as now being distinguished, the *King Arthur's* and the *Leonidas's* and all the other inferiorities cast in the traditional form of the heroic poem.

The second requirement of the epic emerges when we consider the difference we feel between tragedy and epic, a difference simple and fundamental, resting as it does on the original physical conditions governing the two forms. A tragedy is limited in length by the physical comfort of a normal audience. Being serious it will aim at the weightiest effect and it will gain that effect not by crowding everything into a narrow space—that would daze and weary—but by omitting and simplifying. For whatever reason—and the reason is here irrelevant —tragic writers have simplified the local and the transient things and have mainly regarded the most general human passions and the individual's concern with the permanent features of his environment, natural, social, or divine; and by presenting universal experience through the concentrating eye of the individual have been able to turn the limitation of length to the best account. And through that ability acted tragedy has become, as it were, the home country of certain types of feeling—a home country from which colonies have settled in countries where other types of feeling may be characteristic. Thus there is tragic feeling in *Madame Bovary*, but that feeling is not any feeling peculiar to the novel form; it is colonial rather than autochthonous. The peculiar properties of the epic rested, in their turn, on the practical conditions of its performance. Whether a chieftain and his followers in his hall or a band of pilgrims or holidaymakers gathered for some days at a religious festival formed the audience, they wanted or at least tolerated a longer unit than did an audience crowded into the confined space of a theater. On the side of production mere recitation was less exacting than the complication of dramatic circumstance, and, granted relays of reciters, admitted of great length. And the right response to the challenge of length is not repetition but variety.

One of the essentials, therefore, of the epic is abundance and amplitude: great variety of matter, including the widest span of human feelings, ranging if possible from the simple sensualities to a susceptibility to the numinous.

But mere exuberance or range is not enough in itself; and there is a third requirement of the epic: a control commensurate with the amount included. It is this requirement, so crucial to the epic, that can account in recent years for a decline in the status of the long poem as such: a decline which is connected with popular theories on the necessity of the spontaneous element in literature.

It is obvious that in writing a long poem or a long, highly organized work in prose, the composition of which is perforce extended over years, an author cannot sustain a spontaneous vein of creation. At intervals he will be tempted to break the unity of the original conception and stray after new emotional interests. Spontaneity will not suffice to meet the temptation, and the author will have to summon his will to help him abide by the plans he has resolved on. Probably the writing of any poem (except one dictated in dream or trance) needs some effort of the will to control and shape it. But the effort is different in a lyric, a short story, and a play, while only in the most intensely written long works is the will taxed to the utmost. Such sustained writing corresponds to certain phases of the active life. Just as the will may force a man's conduct at a particular time (for instance on an expedition of exploration) to conform to a previously adopted set of resolves, against his present inclinations, so a poet may use his will to suppress new interests and preserve a unity previously resolved on. And the will must have the powerful backing of the reason. The reason has worked on a series of data acquired over a length of time and has been convinced that such-and-such is the right course; and in the crisis the will forces this conviction to override temporary impulses that demand something different.

But in the making of a long poem the will is more than an external driving force; the fact of it and the belief in it become a highly important part of the total experience. Milton speaks of how the Dorian mood of flutes and soft recorders raised

> *To highth of noblest temper Hero's old*
> *Arming to Battel, and in stead of rage*
> *Deliberate valour breath'd.*

But if Milton had never used the phrase " deliberate valour," his belief in the quality of considered courage, aware of issues, which implies the application of the will, would be apparent from the whole trend of his rhetoric. Moreover, in *Paradise Lost*, as in other genuine epics, the very passages which the will has forced into harmony with the more spontaneously composed passages are significant as declaring the fact and the value of the quality to which they owe a large part of their being.

This exercise of the will and the belief in it, which are a corollary of our third epic requirement, help to associate epic poetry with the largest human movements and solidest human institutions. In creating what we call civilization the sheer human will has had a major part. Or think of the institution of marriage. However much spontaneity may enter into it, however truly passion may initiate it, it owes a major part of its existence to the reason; and it could be described not unfairly as a love affair made permanent by the sustained application of the conscious will. And it is marriage the epic resembles, not a passing fancy, or a fierce passion that burns itself out.

The fourth requirement can be called choric. The epic writer must express the feelings of a large group of people living in or near his own time. The notion that the epic is primarily patriotic is an unduly narrowed version of this requirement. Should a country command at some time an exceptionally clear ethical temper, that temper may serve an author well enough. Spenser, for instance, does express the Elizabethan temper successfully in the *Fairy Queen*. But the group-feeling need not be national. Dante is medieval rather than Italian. Indeed, in its simplest and most essential form this requirement may mean that an epic must communicate the feeling of what it was like to be alive at that time. The point is that behind the epic author must be a big multitude of men, of whose most serious convictions and dear habits he is the mouthpiece.

It is in this matter that epic most differs from tragedy. Tragedy cannot lack some imprint of its age, but its nature is to be timeless. It deals with the recurrent human passions and it presents them (having no space to do more) in their bare elements with the least local circumstantiation. It teaches not what it is like to be alive at a certain time but what it is like to be a human being. But though the choric element is necessary to epic and at best adventitious in tragedy, it does not exclude from epic the presentation of those timeless feelings which it is tragedy's privilege to isolate and clarify. Indeed the greatness of epic will partly depend on the inclusion of such feelings. It is when the tragic intensity coexists with the group consciousness of an age, when the narrowly timeless is combined in a unity with the variegatedly temporal, that epic attains its full growth.

I do not intend to insist on the tragic element in epic to the exclusion of others or to assert that it must be the dominant element. The comic element, the way of the world, the subordination of individual caprice to the demands of society, should be there too; and it may greatly preponderate over the tragic without upsetting the epic effect. Other elements, such as romance, satire, fantasy, and the grotesque, can, if not too powerful, contribute to the epic effect and not spoil it; and they can compensate for any lack in the tragic and the comic.

From these four main epic requirements I have tried to describe, one simple fact will follow: that the true epic will assume a form that answers the most serious concerns of any age. When an age has certain opinions about the nature of man, the heroic story may answer the needs. But other forms may suit other ages. The Middle Ages used allegory more seriously than the heroic story, and their most truly epic writings are allegorical. In the nineteenth century the most serious form was prose fiction, and not necessarily with any character so dominant as the hero in the traditional verse epic.

Having explained the suppositions I make in dealing with the epic, I can now proceed to any possible epic writing in the English Middle Ages. In the Homeric age the principal concerns had been the individual at his highest or most intense or most assertive; and they had been presented, quite naturally, through heroic action. The chief successor of Homer as the epic writer of classical antiquity,

Virgil, is a transition figure. He cannot inherit Homer's singleness of mind; he cannot live so intensely and so unquestioningly in the present. But he believes in the civilizing mission of Rome, and so believing can borrow Homer's heroic form in which to express it. But medieval adoration of Virgil was not altogether inept. On the face of it medieval readers did indeed distort him very seriously, for they made the *Aeneid* an allegory of the human soul from birth, symbolized by the shipwreck in the first book, to its final triumph over the vices with the death of Turnus at the end. But it is true that in the course of the poem Aeneas does change from a preponderatingly human figure with rather serious failings into a vast allegorical figure, now almost immune from human weakness and standing for an abstract idea of self-restraint and organized energy. Further, Virgil throughout his poem conveys an otherworldliness that quite separates him from Homer and makes him perfectly appropriate as a chief figure in Dante's *Divine Comedy*. He does therefore mark a transition from the setting of Homer with its this-worldliness, its concern with the dominant individual and what has happily been described as its intense " vertical " light to the medieval setting with its preponderant otherworldliness and its concern with an ideal of holiness to which this or that individual was subordinated. In the medieval setting the heroic poem, though it con-

101

tinued in an unbroken tradition from the end of classical antiquity to its resuscitation in the Renaissance, could not be the dominant form, and its place was taken by the poem which in some form or another described the human soul on its earthly pilgrimage to heavenly salvation. The great continental example of this form is Dante's *Divine Comedy*. Is there any English example?

Since I have extended the epic category to include prose, you may ask whether Malory's *Morte d'Arthur* may not fall within it. I believe not, and especially in view of Vinaver's important conclusions drawn from the recently discovered manuscript at Winchester on which he has based his edition. It now appears that what we believed was one long work is the collected works of Thomas Malory. This discovery both exonerates Malory from the charge of faulty composition, often and quite rightly brought against the work as originally conceived of, and removes him from the small and select class of authors who have staked most of their reputation on a single great work. And when we consider his best work, the sections on Guinevere, the breach between Arthur and Launcelot, and the final battle—the sections that follow the quest of the Grail—we see that the temper is tragic in its concentration and intensity and makes no effort to achieve the epic breadth. These last two sections, the least derivative and the fruit of a long apprenticeship, are very great literature, but they are not relevant to my present theme. Another work that has some outward claim to epic status is Lydgate's version of the French poem of Deguileville on the pilgrimage of human life. There you have the essential subject of medieval epic, but the talented and industrious monk who adapted it to English had neither the ferocity nor the range of mind to begin to approach an epic standard. There is indeed only one work in medieval English that has serious epic pretentions: Langland's *Piers Plowman*. And for this poem I do, quite unequivocally, demand the status of epic; not indeed of flawless epic, but of epic nevertheless.

It is idle to deny Langland's faults of construction. He was obsessed with the sufferings of the poor and with the sins of the rich; and he voices his obsessions in and out of season. There is a major structural tautology in that the opening section, the Vision, which deals with contemporary England in the main, concerns the same active realm of life as the second section, on Do-bet, does. H. W. Wells seeks to prove that these sections concern different portions of the active life and that hence there is no tautology. Technically he may be right in the main; but, in our reading, this technical rightness makes very little difference, and we do not feel a sufficient progression of subject to enable us to grasp these two sections as part of a growing whole. Yet we never quite give up the effort, and even in the most confused sequences we never really doubt that Langland has a clearly formulated end in view. He has ultimately, however much he abuses it, that control of his multifarious material that is essential to the true epic effect. He reminds me of his own parable of the man in the boat. The man may stagger dangerously through the boat's motion, but these staggerings do not interfere with the boat's direction to its goal unless they are such as to force him to neglect the rudder altogether. In the allegory the staggerings are the venial sins, the neglect of the rudder mortal sin. Well, Langland is extremely prone to venial sins of construction; at one point he is near the mortal sin of letting go the rudder altogether: but in the end he steers a straight and magnificent course. I am thinking above all of the masterly evolution leading to the climax. Out of the theme of various trinities emerges the Pauline trinity of Faith, Hope, and Charity. Faith is represented in the person of Abraham, Hope in that of Moses, Charity in that, not of any Old Testament character, but of the Good Samaritan, whose deed of mercy is described. It is then that the progress of the dreamer's mental pilgrimage, one of the main themes of the poem, reaches a definitive point. The dreamer wishes to be enrolled as one of the Good Samaritan's, or Charity's, servants, and his wish is granted. But the Good Samaritan turns out to be another pilgrim, a knight who is on his way to joust in Jerusalem; in other words, Jesus on his way to his final battle with death on the cross. And the old idea of Jesus as the warrior knight is caught up and amplified, when, as Christ the Conqueror of death, he enters Hell and hales out Adam and Eve: the first deed of salvation under the new dispensation. This sequence of changes from the abstract idea of Charity to Christ the Conqueror, the Harrower of Hell, is a sublime display of architectonic power, capable of redeeming a multitude of subordinate lapses.

I have spent most of what space I have available for Langland on this matter of structure, because here he is least sound and most liable to be censured. As for his versification, it is vain to argue. I can only record my impression that Langland's alliterative line is a very flexible medium, able not only to achieve the sententious effect to which alliteration is particularly apt but to cope with sustained thought and exalted feeling. Langland, as in his description of the Four Daughters of God dancing to celebrate the harrowing of Hell all night till the dawning of Easter, can rise to a rapture of which very few English poets are capable. In the matters of variety and of speaking for a large body of men, most would agree that he fulfils these epic requirements. He spans the whole social scale from king to " submerged tenth," and is at home in both tavern and recluse's cell. And he sees his world with the eyes of his age. It may be that he was not personally a

105

sociable man; but that did not prevent him speaking with the voice that thousands recognized as *their* voice. He may have been very much more pious than most of his readers; but that piety of which he may have had more was *their* piety. He had the keenest eye for the things around him; but the things he saw were what his fellows saw, however much more clearly focussed.

I have not spoken at length of the transition from medieval to Renaissance epic, a process in which Lydgate is an important figure. But having briefly mentioned Lydgate in my last chapter and in terms relevant to the development of the epic, I may omit him here. Further, there was no writing in the age of Wyatt and Surrey that had epic pretentions. The *Mirror for Magistrates* in the next epoch is not good enough poetically, and is too narrow in scope, to be taken into account. Nor can any of the translations reach the pitch of autonomous excellence which brings Pope's *Homer* within the epic category. To find anything to compare with *Piers Plowman* as achieved epic, we have to move to the later Elizabethan age, where out of several works of epic pretentions Spenser's *Fairy Queen* and Sidney's *Arcadia* emerge as at least partial successes.

To compare these three works would be a salutary discipline to those who want to minimize the changes between the two epochs. Of course there is a great deal of medievalism in both the Elizabethan works, the *Fairy Queen* especially. Whether or not you can still find in Spenser the four concurrent types of meaning affected by some medieval writers and, according to Nevill Coghill, fundamental to the very skeleton of *Piers Plowman*, I need not try to say. What is certain is that the ebb and flow of the allegory is a medieval inheritance. One of the difficulties and fascinations of the medieval allegory is the problem of how far to push it, how much meaning to see in it. To expect a norm in any one poem is hopeless, because the amount of meaning may shift from place to place in the same poem. And this is exactly the case with Spenser. But this very absence of an allegorical norm is a part of the meaning of the *Fairy Queen*. For the point largely is that we should be kept on the stretch, constantly guessing; that we should make an interpretative effort that will neutralize the narcotic effect of the powerful Spenserian music. And then, further, in the *Fairy Queen* there is the great medieval subject of the pilgrimage. It is found in books one and two and to a lesser extent five; and it is at once a personal pilgrimage to salvation and an evolution much like that found in the different states of Do-wel, Do-bet, and Do-best in *Piers Plowman*. As Do-best combines the ideals of active and contemplative life, so the Red Cross Knight after his ascetic discipline and his vision of New Jerusalem returns to active life to kill the dragon. Yet for all this medievalism there has been

107

a profound change in the *Fairy Queen* from the Middle Ages; and nothing less than a shift of center. In Langland, Holiness is something vast and pervasive, to which the *homunculus* aspires; it is something that dwarfs him. In Spenser, holiness is of the first importance, but it is so as an essential attribute, along with other essential attributes, of a good man, who tends to be not Everyman but one of the ruling class. Spenser was not talking at random when he said that his poem aimed to fashion a gentleman.

In Sidney's *Arcadia* the contrast is even more striking. First, the medievalism is entirely episodic. Sidney does indeed derive a great deal of the substance of his episodes from the medieval romance; but there is nothing to correspond to the allegorical form and pilgrimage subject found in the *Fairy Queen*. The form of the revised *Arcadia*, that is the *Arcadia* universally known till the first version was printed from manuscript in 1926, is purely classical, being derived from a Greek romance constructed on the scheme used by Homer and Virgil. And the substance of *Arcadia*, however much religion there is in it, is essentially the fashioning of gentlemen and gentlewomen by the conspicuous examples of what to perform and what to avoid. Politics are no longer as with Langland an area which should be animated by the great circumambient divine principles but a central activity, of much greater relative size, however strictly to be regulated by religion. Once again the matter is one of position. Please do not take these assertions as forming a final and fixed opinion. If I set out to find more medievalism in *Arcadia* I should succeed. I mainly want to warn you against exaggerating the idea of a continuity between Middle Ages and Renaissance.

In one matter I have pushed ahead too far. I defended Langland's structure in order to forestall objections to his primary right to the epic status. But I have omitted to do the same for the style of *Arcadia*, which many readers, in fact most readers who have tried Sidney in bulk, have found more tedious than they could bear. Now I have to admit that this style has not quite the range to raise *Arcadia* to one of the undoubted epics. Its virtues are amplitude and brilliance and an unflagging vitality. It is the real index of the bravery and gallantry and unsleeping wit of the man. Like the prose of Scott it needs taking fast, but not many readers are sufficiently at home with the periodic structure of most Elizabethan prose to go fast with it and to miss nothing. Once you get to know it and can take it at the right speed you will find that it is flexible as well as vital, capable of far more effects than you ever dreamed, even if it cannot strike the notes of tragedy or prophecy. There cannot be the remotest question of dullness or tedium. It is in fact sufficiently distinguished to allow Sidney to qualify as an epic writer of the second order.

But this matter of Sidney's style in *Arcadia* is only by the way and it does not affect my main plea; which is that both Spenser's verse epic and Sidney's prose epic present at least one major difference from the medieval epic: a great shift of the position of the writer in the realms of the human and the divine. Just as Wyatt had made the lyric more centrally human by introducing drama into it and animating the characters concerned in it, so Spenser and Sidney took up their main position in humanity, however fervently they acknowledged the controlling providence of God. Langland could indeed tell of the life he saw but he could shift his position to realms of abstract holiness in a way impossible to his Elizabethan successors in the epic. And no amount of tracing connections or spotting survivals can alter the magnitude of the change from the one age to the other.

V

Epilogue

I ENDED each of my chapters with a reference to Sidney, and for a special reason. Of all the great writers of the age, Sidney seems to me the most centrally Elizabethan, the one through whom we may most truly interpret the temper of the age. He is at once an inheritor of the past and an innovator. I mentioned first the circumstances of his death; and these showed him the inheritor of the medieval ideal of chivalry and an innovator through his manifesting a new and unmedieval consideration for the individual. I then mentioned a lyric medieval in its question-and-answer form, modern in its dramatic quality, in its sense of the here-and-now, of the speakers being actual, differentiated human beings. I then mentioned the *Defence of Poetry*, and this work combines an inherited religious solemnity with the latest critical news from Italy. My remarks on *Arcadia* do not need recapitulating. It is through a representative figure like Sidney that we can be

111

put on the right way to answer the question that is the subject of these lectures: was there an English Renaissance? Now since I set out to answer this question, you have a right to demand at this stage some not too ambiguous answer. But my words on Sidney suggest that my answer is: there was and there wasn't. And I do not think you should be put off with that. So let me try to state my conclusions, if not more definitely, at least more circumstantially and at slightly greater length than three or four words.

First of all we are viewing a very large area from which the most seemingly contradictory results can be obtained. If you suddenly, as I have done, confront *Piers Plowman* with *Arcadia* you will be struck by the difference: but if you study the *Fairy Queen* through the medieval allegory you will be struck by the likenesses. The best one can do is to try to arrive at a prevailing truth, even if it does not prevail over other truths by a very big margin. With these reservations I conclude that there were certain changes in England that could be called by the name of Renaissance, but that for the most part they came about gradually, with advances and relapses and without the sudden violences of enthusiasm that marked the same movement in Italy. In no art more than in architecture is this contrast apparent. Nothing is more surprising to the observant amateur visiting Italy for the first time than the early date

and the definitive character or some of the classicizing buildings. The break with the Gothic was
sudden and complete. In England classicizing ornament appears hesitatingly in some of the buildings
of the age of Henry VII, like Bishop West's chapel
in Ely Cathedral, and spreads to the funerary monu-
ments. But what a time before Inigo Jones appears!
And even he is almost an anomaly in his age.

> *The sun's rim dips; the stars rush out:*
> *At one stride comes the dark—*

wrote Coleridge of the tropics; and perhaps it is the
influence of our mild and muddled climate with its
prolonged transitions that induced similar prolonga-
tions in the transitions of thought.

We cannot change our climate; so perhaps we
cannot avoid our inconsistencies and blurred transitions. At their worst, these things may be genuinely
annoying and partake of caprice: at their best they
may attain a valuable and peculiar balance, not out
of keeping with the Renaissance ideal of the evenly
developed man. Though the public architecture of
the English Renaissance was muddled, its domestic
architecture (if you include the setting) could attain
a wonderful harmony. I will seek final illustration
from yet another passage of Sidney, this time from
the *Arcadia*, which expresses the genius of English
domestic architecture and of English domestic life at
that time:

113

The house itself was built of fair and strong stone, not affecting so much any kind of fineness as an honorable representing of a firm stateliness. The lights doors and stairs rather directed to the use of the guest than to the eye of the artificer: and yet as the one chiefly heeded, so the other not neglected; each place handsome without curiosity and homely without loathesomeness; not so dainty as not to be trod on, nor yet slubbered up with good fellowship; all more lasting than beautiful but that the consideration of the exceeding lastingness made the eye believe it *was* exceeding beautiful. The servants not so many in number as cleanly in apparel and serviceable in behaviour, testifying even in their countenances that their master took as well care to be served as of them that did serve.

There you have indeed compromise instead of violent and hard contrast; but it is harmonious, not muddled, and it shows what the Renaissance, in its peculiarly English form, was able to accomplish.

Selected References

BELL, CLIVE. *Art.* London, Chatto and Windus, 1931.

DAWSON, CHRISTOPHER HENRY. *Mediaeval Religion and Other Essays.* London, Sheed and Ward, 1934.

HALLER, WILLIAM. *The Rise of Puritanism.* New York, Columbia University Press, 1938.

HULME, T. E. *Speculations.* Edited by Herbert Read. London, Kegan Paul, Trench, Trubner and Co., 1936.

KER, WILLIAM PATON. *Epic and Romance.* London, Macmillan and Co., 1897.

LEWIS, CLIVE STAPLES. *The Allegory of Love.* Oxford, The Clarendon Press, 1936.

MAGNUS, LAURIE. *A General Sketch of European Literature in the Centuries of Romance.* London, Kegan Paul, Trench, Trubner and Co., 1918.

MURRY, JOHN MIDDLETON. *Discoveries, Essays in Literary Criticism.* London, W. Collins and Co., 1924.

OWST, GERALD ROBERT. *Preaching in Medieval Engand.* Cambridge, The University Press, 1926.

PATER, WALTER. *The Renaissance.* Portland, Maine, T. B. Mosher, 1902.

SICHEL, EDITH HELEN. *The Renaissance.* New York, Henry Holt and Co., 1914.

SITWELL, EDITH. *A Poet's Note Book.* London, Macmillan and Co., 1943.

TILLYARD, E. M. W. *The Elizabethan World Picture.* London, Chatto and Windus, 1943.

115

Index

Adams, Henry, *Mont-Saint-Michel* and *Education of Henry Adams:* 7
Allegory in Middle Ages: 100–102
Amplitude, an epic requirement: 95–96
Angelico, Fra: 5
Aquinas, Thomas, on need of recreation: 72–73
Aristotle: as critical kin of Puttenham, 79, 81–83; influence on Sidney's *Defence*, 87
Ascham, Roger, his didacticism: 76–77

Bell, Clive, *Art:* 7–8
Botticelli: 5–6
Bunyan, *Pilgrim's Progress:* 14
Byzantine art, abstraction of: 8–9

Calvinists, English: 20
Caxton, critical importance of his prefaces: 75–76
Chambers, R. W., on Sir T. More: 31
Chaucer: ideal characters of his Knight and Squire, 24–25; both medieval and unique, 26–28; contradiction in, 70; *Nuns' Priest's Tale* as "honest mirth," 72–73
Choric quality of epic: 98–100

Church, medieval, opinion on literature: 71–74
Cimabue: 5
Classical influence in Middle Ages: 74, 79
Commemorative function of literature in Middle Ages: 72
Comparetti, *Virgil in the Middle Ages:* 70
Courtesy: 24–25, 30–34; relation with chivalry, 24–25; includes element of human consideration, 30–34
Critical theory, contradictions in: 70
Cursor Mundi: 72

Dawson, Christopher: 14, 73
Didactic theories of literature: 72, 76–78
Dies irae: 18–20

Elyot, analogy with Surrey: 63
Epic: primitivism in, 92–93; defined, 93–100
Exemplary theories of literature: 77

Gilbert, W. S., *Patience:* 6
Giotto: 5, 8
Gower, representative of age: 30
Greville, Fulke, *Life of Sidney:* 31–33

116